Smoky Mountains
Trout Fishing Guide

Smoky Mountains
Trout Fishing Guide

Don Kirk

Revised Edition

Menasha Ridge Press
Birmingham, Alabama

Ninth Printing, 1998

Cover photo by Joann Kirk
Book design by Teresa Smith

Library of Congress Cataloging-in-Publication Data

Kirk, Don, 1952—
    Smoky mountains trout fishing guide.

    Includes index.
    1. Trout fishing—Great Smoky Mountains National Park (N.C. and
Tenn.)—Guide-books. 2. Great Smoky Mountains National Park (N.C. and
Tenn.)—Guide-books.
I. Title.
SH688.U6K567 1985   799.1'755 83-61709
ISBN 0-89732-036-0

Menasha Ridge Press
P. O. Box 43059
Birmingham, AL 35243
(800) 247-9437
www.menasharidge.com

Contents

Foreword

In 1983 the first printing of Don Kirk's book hit the stores around the Great Smoky Mountains National Park. *Smoky Mountains Trout Fishing Guide* has evidently been a hit since only two years later I find myself writing another foreword to the revised edition. In that short period of time many things have changed.

Don is no longer a novice writer timidly approaching the publication of his first few magazine articles and a book. He is now a seasoned pro with a string of writing credits spanning all the outdoor magazines of any note in the country. He has begun work on his second book, this time dealing with the Tennessee Valley Authority lakes, and he has taken over possession of my canoe, for which he will never be properly forgiven.

The first edition of this book leaned heavily toward the Tennessee side of the Park, due to the fact that he and I both live in the Volunteer State and are inordinately proud of the fact. He is a resident by accident of birth; me, as a born-again Yankee, through accident of fate. In this version you will find far more information on streams in North Carolina's piece of the Smokies and, as a bonus, advice on fishing the several lakes gracing the outskirts of this half million acres of Appalachian wilderness.

Between the pages of this book still lies the best collection of information in existence on fishing this national park. What Don said three years ago at this writing still holds, and if you and I do our job in curbing acid rain, maintaining the inviolable nature of our national park system, and maintaining our wise stewardship of the land, it will still hold in 30 years when his kids, mine, and maybe yours will be wading the freshets that are an integral part of our community.

Three years ago, it seemed proper to me to be introducing you to Don. Now I'm not so sure. While professionally I had a bit of a head start, he has certainly surpassed me in his output and enthusiasm for communicating through the written word.

Once again I'll cut this foreword short for two reasons. First, I'm relatively sure no one reads this drivel, and second, if you do you are really wasting time that could be spent several more pages into the book learning the secrets of the Smoky Mountains trout water and enjoying Don's companionship.

Look for us both on the lakes and streams of the park; we'll be the ones with two cameras apiece.

Marc Sudheimer
Lakeside–Cherokee
June 15, 1985

Acknowledgments

This book is the result of several years of effort. Many hours were spent poring over old Park records and maps and conducting interviews to insure depth and accuracy. Without the aid and support of a number of people, this project could not have been completed.

All National Park Service personnel contacted were very helpful. In particular, Stewart (Stu) Coleman gave generously of his time and provided essential information. Alan Kelley of the U.S. Fish and Wildlife Service furnished material on brook trout and the Cades Cove area. Robert Smith, also of the U.S. Fish and Wildlife Service, supplied technical data and research tips. Uplands Laboratory's Ray Matthews provided information concerning Abrams Creek; and Steve Moore of Uplands Laboratory was kind enough to review the book's outline.

Technical information on feeding habits of the trout of the area was provided by Price Wilkinson, fishery biologist for the Tennessee Wildlife Resource Agency. Price also checked the outline of the book. Good friend and fishing buddy Marc Sudheimer, also of the TWRA, contributed encouragement that kept the typewriter ribbon moving and capped the project by writing the foreword.

Dr. David Etnier of the Department of Zoology at the University of Tennessee looked over my outline and furnished valuable information on caddis flies.

Much of the historical background could never have been assembled without the cooperation of a number of fine folks from western Carolina and eastern Tennessee. Space does not permit the mention of all who contributed, but among those who must be mentioned is Walter Cole of Gatlinburg. Walter spent a warm morning in May with me on his front porch telling me of the mountains and the men of his youth. Ernest Ramsey of Pigeon Forge provided me with a wealth of information concerning his years spent guiding fishermen in the Smokies, building split cane rods and tying flies. Jack Shuttle, owner of a tackle shop in Newport, tied and explained a score of Smoky Mountain flies for me. Wendell Crisp, a Bryson City tackle shop owner, also provided information on North Carolina fly patterns and shared his memories of the old days when he was a boy living in Proctor. Kirk Jenkins of Newport provided me with a number of superbly tied Yallarhammars and Little River Ants, as well as vital stream information. Jim Ellison of Morristown shared the tactics and flies he developed for fishing such difficult waters as Greenbriar. Jim Mills, a top-notch fly tier and fly fisherman, also assisted in my research.

Mr. Olin Watson, president of the Smoky Mountains Historical Society, was kind enough to share some tales recalled from the days he hunted and fished the ridges of the Smokies.

Information concerning the Cherokee Indians was furnished by Duane King, director of the Museum of the Cherokee Indians, and Adam Thompson, stocking coordinator for the Cherokee Fish and Game Management Enterprise.

Tom Justie, Sam Venerable, and my son Jeff Kirk accompanied me on several photographic trips in the Park. George Keener assisted with advice on photographic problems.

My sincere thanks to all who gave of their time, expertise, and knowledge to the compilation of this book.

Introduction

The Great Smoky Mountains National Park offers one of the last wild trout habitats in the eastern United States. Annually millions of Americans visit this natural wonderland seeking recreation and a chance to enjoy the outdoors. Among these visitors are thousands of anglers eager to test their luck against the streambred trout of the Park's famed waters. Most lack the needed information and are confused by the seemingly endless number of streams available.

This book is designed to help both experienced and novice anglers select waters that suit their tastes and abilities. You'll find a chapter on each of the major streams in the Park. Listed with each stream will be such valuable data as its location, fishing pressure, species of trout found in that particular watershed, both auto and trail access routes, campsite accommodations, and other information. Also included are chapters covering the early history of trout fishing in the Park, information on the aquatic insects that are most abundant in the streams, proven dry and wet nymph patterns, tips on gear, spinner fishing, etc. In the Great Smoky Mountains National Park, we have some of the finest trout fishing anywhere. Though trout are wary, even a beginner can expect to catch a few.

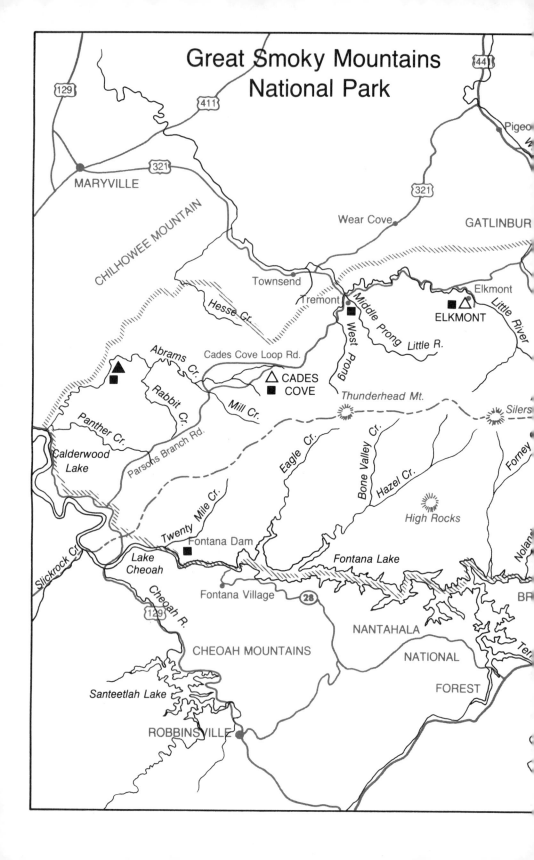

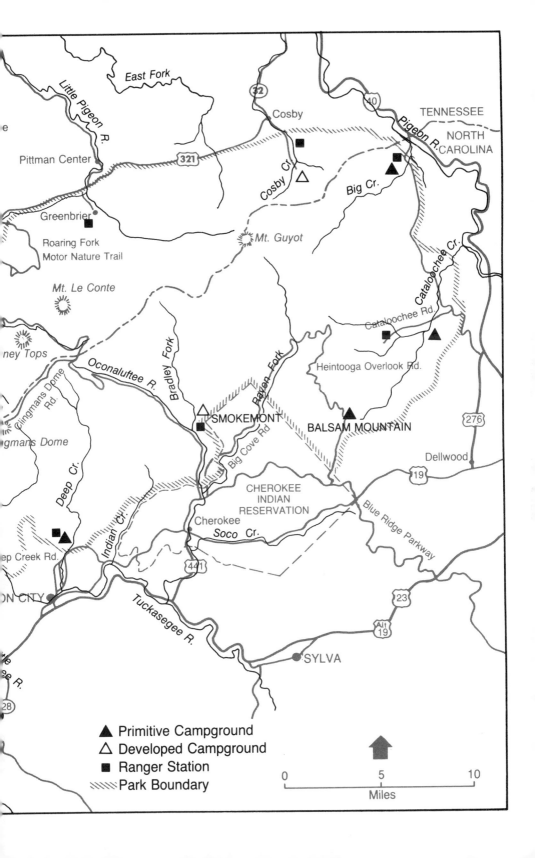

Smoky Mountains Trout

The majestic Great Smoky Mountains National Park is a rugged half-million-acre wilderness sanctuary located on the common border of Tennessee and North Carolina. Encompassed in the Park are numbers of steep, tree-lined ridges, separated by deep valleys. There are over seven hundred miles of cool, crystal-clear streams.

One of the most diverse biospheres on earth, the Smokies range from an elevation of 850 feet at the mouth of Abrams Creek to 6,642 feet on Clingmans Dome. Flora is incredibly broad, with several trees reaching their record growth in the Park. There are 13 major watersheds in the Smokies, as well as a number of smaller ones. These streams range in size from the largest, Little River and Oconaluftee River, which during periods of normal flow are big enough to float a canoe down, to an almost endless number of small headwater rills. Living in these streams is a wide spectrum of aquatic insects and invertebrates, as well as more than 70 species of fish, including darters, suckers, dace, shiners, chubs, sculpins, bream, bass, and the native brook trout. Since the turn of the century, two other species, the rainbow and brown trout, have become a part of the ecosystem of the Smokies, although they are considered "exotics" by fisheries biologists.

The Brook Trout (*Salvelinus fontinalis*)

The brook trout, known affectionately to the mountain folk of the Smokies as the "spec," is not a true trout, but a char. The world's trout, salmon, grayling, and whitefish are members of one homogenous group. The trout, in turn, are divided into two technically separate groups, the true trout and the chars.

This classification is arrived at principally through skeletal structure, teeth, and scale differences. This is of little importance to anglers, as the more apparent differences in coloration are obvious. Chars always have a dark background color with light spots. True trout, such as the rainbow and brown, always have a light background color with dark spots.

The brook trout is distinctive from other fish with its "wormlike" markings on its back (known as vermiculations) and white-edged lower fins. The brook trout, like all chars, spawns in the fall.

In the Smokies the brook trout feed on numerous forms of aquatic insects including stone flies, mayflies, and caddis flies. Terrestrial insects also play an important part of their diet and include bees, wasps, beetles, ants, jassids, flies, and grasshoppers. Crayfish are important daily fare, as are minnows. The brook trout is capable of digesting a stomachful of food in less than half an hour, a fact that prods the brookie to stay on constant lookout for morsels of most any type.

The brookies of the Smokies were "marooned" here after the glacial epoch. Originally an ocean-dwelling fish from the Arctic, the brook trout migrated down the Eastern seacoast, fleeing the freezing onslaught of the ensuing Ice Age. When the rivers had cooled sufficiently to offer suitable habitat, the brookies moved upstream, establishing themselves. As the rivers began to warm, the brook trout were forced to retreat into the cool mountain headwaters.

The brook trout was once abundant in the Smokies. Accounts of fishing trips made into these mountains prior to 1890 tell of fish being caught by the hundreds. Large-scale logging operations came into the Smokies in the late 1890s. Whole watersheds were logged out, dams were erected on the streams, railroad lines were built up alongside many streams, and fires feeding on the slash left behind by the timber-cutting operations were but some of the devastating problems the remaining brook trout faced. All logging operations ceased in 1935 (approximately two-thirds of the Smokies were logged during this period) and better land management helped heal the wounds of the previous 40 years.

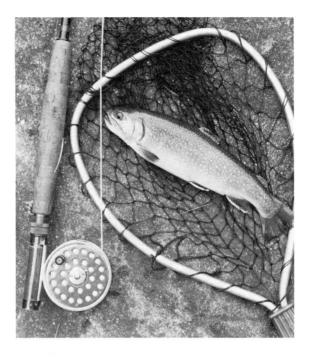

A brook trout. Photo by Don Kirk.

Rainbow trout were introduced into every major stream in the Smokies during this period. Massive stockings of rainbow trout were continued through 1947. The brook trout, which lost over half its original range to the loggers, is now losing additional territory to the rainbow trout. Why the brook trout cannot regain its lost range where habitat conditions have returned to near normal, and what part the rainbow trout plays in this drama, is not fully understood. Several explanations have been offered, and research into the dilemma continues. A moratorium was placed on the killing of brook trout in the Park in 1975. Scores of headwater streams were closed (and remain so at this writing) to protect the remaining brookies.

The Rainbow Trout *(Salmo gairdneri)*

The very name of this fish rings out with a surge of raw energy and beauty. The rainbow is well known for unsurpassed fighting ability, arching leaps, and superb eating quality. A powerful downstream run by one of these fish that rips the line from your reel will make you feel as if your heart is trying to bypass your Adam's apple.

The rainbow trout's original range extended from California to Bristol Bay in Alaska. This fish prefers fast, oxygenated water. Recognizable by its silvery flanks slashed with scarlet and its greenish back, the rainbow is a beautiful fish. Predominately an insect eater, particularly in the streams of the Smokies, the rainbow will, however, strike spinners and minnow imitations with gusto.

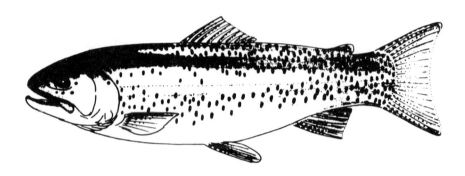

Rainbow trout from the Sierra Mountains of California were shipped to Michigan in 1878. In a few years the adaptable western natives were providing blue ribbon fishing on a number of Michigan rivers. Sportsmen across the eastern part of the country sought the highly touted rainbow to replace the quickly diminishing brook trout. Rainbows were easily reared in hatcheries, but proved to be discontented in small streams when suitable habitat in larger waters was open to them. The wanderlust problem is of little concern to fisheries personnel in the Southern Appalachian Mountains, where the fish are confined to small streams and rivers (except for a few high-elevation impoundments).

Rainbow trout are spring spawners, with runs normally beginning in February. An interesting change has been observed recently in Southern rainbows, with a few fish spawning in the fall. I have caught rainbows from the West Prong of the Little Pigeon in October and early November that were decked out in dark spawning hues and full of roe.

The exact date and site of the first stocking of rainbow trout in the Smokies is not known. There is some contention that landowners stocked them in Abrams Creek in 1900, though no records were kept. Today, the rainbow trout is the dominate gamefish in the Park, having extended its range into every stream system.

Most fish average 7 inches in length, with an occasional nice size 'bow taken. On rare days three- to four-pound fish are caught. Spawning runs from impoundments (Fontana, Cheoah, and Chilhowee lakes) often bring large fish upstream for short periods of time, but this usually occurs in late December through February.

The Brown Trout (*Salmo trutta*)

The brown trout was brought to this country from Germany in 1883. Eggs shipped across the Atlantic arrived at a New York hatchery, where they were hatched and planted in local waters. Brown trout stock from Scotland arrived the following year. Fish from the German strain were called German browns or Von Behr trout, and those from Scotland were known as Loch Leven browns. For a number of years records listed the two fish individually. Today, however, all *Salmo trutta* in this country are referred to as simply brown trout.

Brown trout were introduced into the Tennessee Valley in 1900. Browns in excess of 25 pounds have been caught in this region, and the largest known brown taken in the Park was a respectable 16 pounder. Although browns were never stocked in the Smokies, downstream waters were stocked by both Tennessee and North Carolina fish and game agencies in the 1950s. Browns had begun appearing in the waters of the Park in the early 1960s, and by 1977 brown trout occupied over 50 miles of Park waters.

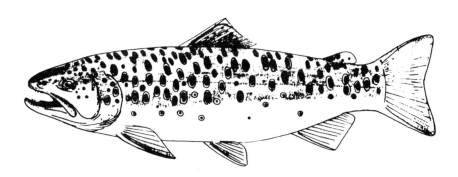

Brown trout are primarily insect eaters, with adult mayflies being their favorite food. Halford, the famous English angling writer, wrote of the feeding habits of the brown trout: "The nymphs are the brown trout's beef, and the adult mayfly his caviar." A carnivorous creature, the brown will utilize everything in a stream, from tiny plankton to an occasional brother or sister. In Park streams larger members of this clan are

A nice three-and-a-half-pound Smoky Mountains brown trout. Photo by Joann Kirk.

nocturnal in feeding. The best time to tie into a big brown in the Smokies is at dusk or dawn, or right after a rain.

The brown trout can be distinguished by its generally brownish-yellow color with orange spots on the sides—although a few are sometimes a silverish tan with dark brown spots. Brown trout prefer slower water than do rainbows, but have been taken in fast waters up to 4,500 feet elevation in Park streams. These fish are fall spawners.

Trout Fishing
in the Smokies

The story of trout fishing in the Great Smoky Mountains and surrounding regions has been largely ignored in print. Whether for sport or sustenance, fishing has long been a favorite American pursuit. Trout fishing in the crystal-clear waters of the Smokies has occupied a special place in the fabric of mountain life since before the arrival of the settlers.

The Cherokee Indians were perhaps the first people to encounter the local brook trout. The Cherokee name for these colorful little fish was "Unahnvsahti." For the Cherokee, fishing was not a recreational pastime, though it was not altogether an arduous affair.

Brook trout served as trail fare for Indian travelers crossing the rugged mountains. A favorite and very effective method of getting trout was to sprinkle a pool or two with poison made from local plants. After being stricken by the poison, the fish, which were usually stunned, floated to the surface and were easily gathered.

The use of a weir was another fishing technique employed by the Cherokees for capturing brook trout and other fish. A "v" of rocks was positioned in a stream. At the point of the "v" a weir was fastened down. Fish were driven downstream and caught in the weir. This sort of effort was often a cooperative undertaking by several families or even an entire village. A community fish fry usually followed.

Early settlers arriving in the Tennessee Valley found the cloud-covered peaks mantled in the most diverse hardwood forest in the world. Preferring to carve a living out of the many rich river bottoms, most bypassed the Smokies. Those that chose to live in the isolated mountains picked the rich coves and scattered bottomland. As the population grew, some settlers moved westward, while others moved farther up the slopes of the mountains in search of tillable land. Travel was difficult, and hard cash was as scarce as "hen's teeth." The region became a backwater area in America's great western movement of the nineteenth century. It

7

developed its own distinct culture, independent and self-reliant, whose colorful life-style flourished for almost a century.

The mountain folks, like the Cherokees, looked upon the brook trout as a dependable source of food rather than sport. Referred to as "specs" by these mountaineers, brook trout originally prospered above an elevation of 2,000 feet. The hardworking mountain people must surely have enjoyed fishing for these game little fighters. Early accounts repeatedly speak of daily catches of hundreds of fish. Fishing methods such as poisoning and weirs were adopted from the Cherokee.

One favorite method commonly used in this region was known as "choking." Fish hooks were out of the reach of the economically depressed mountain people, but their resourcefulness sidestepped this problem neatly. A suitable bait was tied to a length of string and dropped into the water. When a trout would take, the trick was to quickly jerk the fish out onto the bank before it had a chance to expel the bait. According to old-timers, many a meal of fresh trout came to the table as a result.

Logging in the Smokies prior to the 1880s was insignificant compared to what the land endured during the next 55 years. The abundant forests of the Southern mountains had not escaped the attention of a growing nation's appetite for wood. Big-time logging operations descended upon the Southern Appalachians near the close of the nineteenth century. The shrill sound of the narrow gauge locomotives laboring up steep grades could be heard from northern Virginia to Georgia. The Smokies, situated in the middle of this widespread activity, yielded over a billion board feet of lumber by 1935.

These cuttings devastated both the land and the wildlife. The brook trout, which requires unpolluted, cold water, could not cope with silt-choked streams, high water temperatures, dams, and other factors. Concerned fishermen shipped in rainbow trout in the early 1900s. The adaptable rainbow prospered. Anglers of that era contend that fishing during the first 30 years of this century was the best ever seen in these mountains. The streams were free of overhead cover. Many forms of aquatic insects prospered in the sunlight. Open glades, then common alongside many streams, were working alive with grasshoppers, the favorite summer bait of that time. Trout were said to have averaged over a pound apiece.

Walter Cole, a resident of Gatlinburg now in his late nineties, was born in the Sugarland and roamed the Smokies before the arrival of the logging companies. He shared these memories with me one morning in 1980:

"As I remember, I was seven years old when my father and older brother allowed me to come along when they crossed over Blanket Mountain, by the Huskey Gap Trail, to fish for trout in Little River. We packed in our cornmeal, skillet, lard, coffee, blankets, axe, and gun. We had our crop laid in, with harvesting time still a ways off. In those days anybody could just go up in the mountains, build a shelter, and stay as long as they wanted, huntin' and fishin'.

"The logging people hadn't come yet and the creeks were swarming with speckle trout, thick as gnats. It was always dark as sundown, fishin' for them, with the big hemlocks and poplars shadin' out the light. It was easy to catch all the 10- to 14-inch fish you wanted then. I've even caught a few that were a tad longer than 16 inches.

"We set up camp and gathered enough stickbait to last all day, then cut us a good birch sapling for a fishin' pole. We started up the creek stringing our catch on a stick till it wouldn't hold another fish. We set it down in a deep pool to keep it cool, moving on upstream doing the same till we had caught all we wanted. On the way back to camp we collected the hidden fish, fried them whole in hot grease, and ate them with nothin' except cornbread. That was the best eatin' I ever had. We would do that every summer, sometimes staying for weeks living on fish and game we'd sometimes shoot. Come frost we'd be sure to be home to get in the corn and cut wood."

Cole later went to work for the Little River Logging Company, where he did a bit of everything. He recalled the riotous living in the Elkmont camp where moonshine, gambling, fast women, and fishing were as much a part of living as sawdust and splinters. "I was there when the first rainbow trout came into camp from Michigan. They raised them up in a run next to Little River. When they were ready to release them in the creeks, they turned half of them loose in Little River and hauled the others over Huskey Gap, by a mule-pulled wagon, in rain barrels, to the West Prong of the Little Pigeon. I believe the year was 1911. The fishery people have been trying to figure out what has driven the 'specs' off. I can tell you in one word, rainbow. The brook trout's time has passed. Someday I figure the rainbow may have to give way to the brown trout, just the same way."

During these years the Smokies began to attract the attention of serious anglers. Some were sport fishermen whose lines were tipped with a feathery fly; others preferred to cast dynamite into a pool. The American angling scene, which during the late 1860s had seen the introduction of bright colored flies for trout, was undergoing a change of its own during these times. An angler from New York, Theodore Gordon, was experimenting with a new technique for taking trout. Correspondence between Gordon and F. M. Halford, an Englishman, dubbed the "father of dry fly fishing," led to Halford's sending Gordon a sample of English dry flies. From this beginning the sport of dry fly fishing spread from Gordon's home waters in the Catskills down the Appalachian range. In the Southern Appalachians, however, it was not nearly as quickly embraced as in many other regions.

Most early anglers of the South used the old "buggy whip" style

Dan Whitehead stocking a mountain stream. Photo by Don Pfitzer.

rods—or a simple cane pole. The buggy whip rods were sometimes homemade from such materials as ash, hickory, or cherry. Hair from the tail of a stallion or gelding was used to make fishing line. (Many experienced fishermen shunned the use of hair from a mare or filly because it was believed that contact with urine weakened the strength of the fibers.) Most Appalachian trout fishermen lacked the funds to purchase the five-dollar Charles F. Orvis flyrods, or even the one-dollar bamboo rods pictured in the large mail-order catalogs. There was at least one local rod builder, located in Pigeon Forge. The Ramsey Rods, built completely from scratch, lacked the exquisite craftsmanship of the shops of the East; yet they exhibited a fine feel and were affordable. Those that remain today are treasured by their owners.

Each little community had its own group of devoted hunters and fishermen. These fellows spent an enormous amount of time hunting bear or raccoon and fishing. Having a reputation for being in the mountains at all hours was also useful to those making moonshine. The phrase "going fishing" often implied one was going to brew "corn squeezins." I sometimes wonder if trout, which are fond of sweet corn, did not develop this taste during the days of moonshine making, when mash was commonly dumped in the streams!

Trout fishing gradually shifted from a matter of catching trout for supper to catching trout for recreation. The use of bait slowly gave way to the use of artificials. Each streamshed of the Smokies had at least a couple of men in those days who could be hired out as guides for fishing, hiking, or hunting, as the era of the traveling hunter/fisherman was becoming popular nationwide.

Robert S. Masonin in his now out-of-print book *The Lure of the Smokies*, published in 1927, devoted several pages to fishing in the Smoky Mountains. He listed the names of guides who were available for hire, flies most effective, and comments from a number of long-time anglers of this region.

Matt Whittle, a Gatlinburg horticulturalist by trade, fished the streams of the Smokies all his life and was perhaps the best known angler on the Tennessee side of the mountains. Christened the "Izaak Walton" of the Smokies, Whittle understood the habits of his quarry as few have. Going against the common belief of his day that indicated matching the hatch when fishing with flies, Whittle felt it was of no real importance what kind of fly you used, but how you fished with what you were using and how the fish were feeding. Whittle often left his shrubbery business to guide "Yankee" fishermen up the streams of the Smokies. Well-known angler George LeBranche was said to have been among those who accompanied Whittle into the Smokies.

The Hazel Creek area was one of the most developed regions of the Smokies prior to the formation of the National Park. It was also the stomping ground of Col. Calhoun and the well-known Hazel Creek Club. From their lodge, which was located on Hazel Creek near the present-day Calhoun backcountry campsite, members hunted boar, bears, and deer during the winter and fished for trout during the summer. Tales of the exploits of these rough-and-ready men and their favorite hounds are still the subject of lively discussions among locals.

One of the most famous duos of the mountains were two North Carolina mountain men named Samuel Hunnicutt and Mark Cathey. Natives of the Bryson City/Deep Creek area, they were said to have been inseparable companions, from the turn of the century through the 1920s. Deep Creek, which they considered the best fishin' in the country, was a favorite haunt of both. Cathey occasionally undertook the chore of guiding fishermen into the Smokies. He accompanied Horace Kephart up Deep Creek on a number of his many trips. Kephart, aside from being one of the earliest outdoor scribes to give accounts of the Smokies and an outspoken advocate for the formation of the National Park, was fond of trout fishing in these mountains. Cathey took considerable satisfaction in allowing his guest to watch him bewitch trout using his "dance of the fly." Using a long cane pole, he would dabble the fly over the water in a figure eight, enticing even the most wary and sullen trout into a vicious strike.

Hunnicutt and Cathey would spend weeks at a time on the upper reaches of Deep Creek. An amusing tale concerning one of their trips tells of the two leaving camp at the forks of the Left Prong and the mainstream of Deep Creek early one morning. Cathey was to fish the Left Prong until supper and Hunnicutt the Right. Hunnicutt found the fish less than cooperative and returned to camp empty-handed. Cathey had not yet made it back, so after waiting for a while, Hunnicutt decided to try his hand up the Left Prong and meet Cathey on his return trip. He'd fished approximately 300 yards of the creek, creeling 11 nice trout along the way, when he rounded a bend and saw Cathey, who had 90 trout strung over his shoulder. Hunnicutt asked Cathey if he was mad about his coming to meet him. Cathey's reply was short and rather stern as he eyed the 11 fish at Hunnicutt's side: "No, but had you not come to meet me, I would have had a hundred trout when I reached camp."

Carl Standing Deer, of the Qualla Reservation, was perhaps the best known sport angler among the Cherokees during the early years of the National Park. Standing Deer, whose greatest call to fame rested on his deadly aim with his hand-built bow, proudly referred to himself as the grandson of Suyetta, the revered Cherokee storyteller. Standing Deer was a dyed-in-the-wool traditionalist, used horsehair lines after gut and even nylon lines were available, and scorned flies, preferring stickbait and wasp larvae. Standing Deer considered Deep Creek to have the finest fishing in the Smokies and was occasionally available as a guide.

After the National Park was formed the fishing changed. Gradually bait fishing became illegal in all Park waters. Creel and size limits were imposed. Auto access to many streams became a thing of the past. With the building of Fontana Dam, the Park grew as the TVA turned over much of the land it had acquired from residents who would have been isolated as a result of the impounding of the Little Tennessee River. The power from Fontana Dam was funneled into the nation's secret atomic research center at Oak Ridge. The Smokies were the site of some secret road-building practice for the Army Corps of Engineers and of other experiments for the wartime military.

Until 1947 the streams of the Smokies were annually stocked with large numbers of both brook and rainbow trout in an effort to provide Park visitors with "quality" fishing. Rearing stations were operated at the Chimneys, Tremont, Cades Cove, and on Kepharts Prong. Today the Smokies offer fine sport fishing for rainbow and brown trout. Fishing for brook trout was sharply curtailed in 1975, when a large number of brook trout streams were closed to all fishing and it then became illegal to kill a brook trout.

This area is rich in tradition and fishing tales. When tramping down the banks of these streams, it is always interesting to wonder what happened along these trails during past years.

Fishing Tactics
and Helpful Tips

Angling for Smokies trout is not limited to expert fishermen. Trout can be caught on a two-dollar cane pole or on a two-hundred-dollar boron flyrod. Fine fishing tackle is a joy to use, but by no means is it a prerequisite to success astream. The name of the game is having fun.

Several important bits of information will aid in catching trout. An angler increases his chances if he knows where his quarry prefers to "hang out" and what morsels are most tempting to his palate. Other important keys to success include mastering a stealthy approach to the stream and being able to place your offering in a spot that will not alarm the fish.

Each of the three trout of the Smokies tends to occupy slightly different water when feeding, although any one species may occasionally be in any given spot. Trout in the wild have established feeding spots or stations where they position themselves to await food coming down with the current. Size and aggressiveness determine how good a feeding spot a trout is able to defend and keep.

Understanding where trout position themselves in the stream is one of the most important bits of knowledge an angler can possess. When surveying a pool or stretch of pocket water for likely fish-holding spots, remember a trout must have cover that shields it from the current and offers at least limited shelter during times of danger. A typical pool starts with a noisy waterfall. The water rushes over smooth gray boulders, falling into a carved-out plunge pool. Current-loving rainbow trout are right at home in the swift waters of the plunge pool. Large rainbow trout often station themselves at the base of the falls, while smaller members of the clan will gather around the perimeter of the pool or in the pool's main channel. From the depths of the plunge pool the flow of the stream moves on to the tail of the pool, where the average depth becomes more shallow. It is here you will often find the secretive brown trout. His favorite lairs are near solitary rocks or submerged tree roots alongside the bank. These fish, particularly the large fellows, often shun feeding during the daylight hours, preferring to chase minnows at night. Brook trout favor much the same sort of habitat as the brown trout, though the brookie does not shy away from a sunlit meal. Pocket water, so common to the Park, can be treated like a miniature pool.

Where fish are located is important, but of equal importance is their feeding habits. The trout of the Park are best termed as "opportunistic feeders." The streams of the Smokies and surrounding mountains are poor producers of food; they are on the acidic side and carry only a limited amount of nutrients (Abrams Creek is the only notable exception). While by no means barren of aquatic insects, local streams do not support the massive concentrations of the spring run limestone creeks of Pennsylvania or Hampshire, England. A typical trout will, in the course of a few hours, consume a combination of mayflies, caddis flies, stone flies, midges, and a terrestrial or two. A close examination of their stomach contents will reveal dominate feeding on the most abundant food, but along with that particular food, a few other tidbits will usually be present. During the late winter and very early spring Smokies trout feed primarily on the nymphs.

Spring is a time of brisk activity in and on the streams. As the season progresses, the weather becomes milder, warming the water. Insect emergence becomes more common, along with surface feeding of trout. Such activity peaks by late spring, about the only time local trout can afford to be selective, so fly selection should be considered. Terrestrials quickly become important to the diet of the trout, even in spring.

Summer fishing action is often slow. The remaining insect hatches are small and sporadic. Streams suffer from the seasonal dry weather, often running at little more than a trickle, compared to a couple of months earlier. Water temperatures rise, causing many trout to seek deep, cool havens and to feed at night. Successful anglers often use terrestrial imitations such as grasshoppers, ants, jassids, beetles, caterpillars, and bees.

Fall is an exciting time. The scenery surrounding the streams is at its best. Trees and shrubs are decked out in their most daring bright yellows, flame reds, spectacular oranges, and regal golds. Trout seem to sense the coming winter, and feed with uncharacteristic abandon. Terrestrials are still the cornerstone of their diets, though often overlooked are some interesting hatches of caddis flies. During late fall, feeding on growing nymphs and larvae takes on increasing importance.

The winter months find trout reacting to the cold water by becoming torpid and holding close to the bottom. The cold water slows down the fish's metabolism, reducing the amount of food needed to survive. Anglers feeling the urge to fish during the winter will be pleased to learn that on the mild days, trout move into the sunny areas and do a modest amount of feeding.

Armed with an understanding of where the trout are and having a good idea of their food, the angler can use his knowledge on the stream. The importance of a quiet approach and accurate presentation of his lure or fly cannot be overemphasized. Try as best as you can to avoid getting in a hurry. Stand back for a minute to observe and plan a strategy. The fish are usually facing upstream, into the current. Most experienced Smoky Mountains trout fishermen prefer to fish upstream, thus coming up behind their quarry. Exceptions to this would be in times of high or cloudy water. Unless you are an expert caster, chances are you will not place every cast in the desired spot, but if you can hit the right spot with the right offering often enough, you will catch fish.

The question is often asked, "What is the best way to fish the streams of the Park—fly-fishing, spinners, or what?" The simplest and least expensive method for having a productive day on one of the creeks of the Smokies is to incorporate the use of a simple cane pole. Use of cane poles was widespread in the Smokies prior to World War II, and it is still fairly common to encounter an old fisherman from Bryson City or Cosby fishing with a 10- to 14-foot pole. The mountain folk are awesomely deadly with these.

Besides being very effective, cane poles are one of the least expensive routes you can take. An out-of-state visitor who forgets his fishing gear and wants to try his luck on Park waters can purchase a pole, spool of four-pound test line, a half dozen flies, and a fishing permit for under $15.

A cane pole enables you to stand back from the area where the fly is dropped. Tactics employed when using a cane pole are almost the same as those used when fly-fishing, and the basics are the same for a wet fly, dry, or nymph. Attempt to drop the fly along the edges of waterfalls, allowing the current to carry it to the end of the pool or run. If a strike does not occur the first time and you feel there is a fish in the area, repeat the drift in a slightly different section of the pool. It is advisable to keep a tight line the entire time your fly is on or in the water, as a lightning-fast strike can occur at any point.

Fly fishermen will find that that the biggest obstacle to ideal fishing conditions is the lack of casting room, plus problems with drag. You will find yourself doing a good deal of sidearm casting, especially on some of the small streams. Plan to lose a few flies while angling these canopied streams.

Drag problems will depend on the sort of water you are attempting to challenge. If you cast to water that has few crosscurrents, or limit yourself to extremely short casts, drag will be minimal. If you prefer to make long casts across broken pocket water, or exposed rocks, you will be forced to mend line constantly. Those proficient casters attempting the long shots into distant feedling lanes, across such previously mentioned barriers, who are experienced in dealing with an every-constant drag problem will catch considerably more fish. When concentrating your efforts on short, easy casts, you risk getting close enough to the fish to alert them of your presence.

Picking an ideal flyrod for the streams of the Smokies is a job comparable to picking the ideal wine. Long flyrods (9–9.5 feet) have been the choices of a number of highly successful, longtime patrons of the region; but an almost equal number of noted fly fishermen prefer extremely short flyrods (6–6.5 feet).

Those favoring the long rod say the added length allows them to keep more line off the water, thus helping to eliminate drag. Greater casting accuracy is also cited as a plus for the long rod.

The school which favors short rods cites the use of light lines (#3 to #4) and maneuverability on the stream as solid advantages. The short rod is easy to work on small streams, where overgrowth can hinder casting.

Fly fishermen may be the classic attention-getters of the trout streams, but the spinner fishermen account for more trophy trout. Chasing after tiny insects might satisfy smaller fish, but a large fish may have to expend more energy on an insect than can be derived from its consumption. For this reason large trout depend on minnows, crayfish, and even smaller trout for their daily fare.

There are several successful methods of fishing the streams of the Smokies with spinners. Most experienced spinner specialists prefer to concentrate their efforts on the large- to medium-size streams. On long, slow pools, common to the lower reaches of many creeks in the Park, the trick is to stand below the pool you wish to fish and cast upstream. Retrieve the lure at a pace slightly faster than the speed of the current. Work upstream, retrieving your lure at various speeds and depths. When you get within casting distance of the head of the pool, attempt casts to both sides of the falls, allowing the lure to sink before actively retrieving. These basic tactics can be adapted to small streams or broken pocket water.

Spinning outfits must be built to cast light lures accurately. Current fishing regulations prohibit the use of lures and plugs with more than one hook. Single-hook regulations are becoming more common across the nation each year. But single-hook lures can sometimes be difficult to locate on short notice. The largest maker of single-hook lures, Mepps, markets a wide variety of spinning lures in different colors, designs, and sizes of the finest construction. Anglers unable to locate any single-hook spinners can take a pair of pliers and cut all but one hook from available lures, making them perfectly legal.

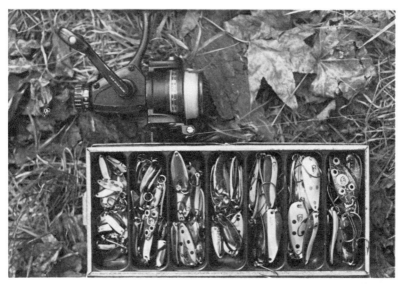

Single-hook spoons are deadly on Great Smoky Mountains National Park trout. Photo by Joann Kirk.

License Requirements and Park Fishing Regulations

Either a North Carolina or Tennessee license entitles the angler to fish anywhere within the Park boundaries.

Copies of current fishing regulations may be obtained at the Sugarlands Visitors Center, located two miles south of Gatlinburg, in the Park, or by writing the Superintendent of the Great Smoky Mountains National Park, 107 Park Headquarters Road, Gatlinburg, TN 37738, or call (423) 436-1200.

Stream Insects and
Feathery Flies

Aquatic insects in the Smokies streams play an essential role in the diet of the trout. Fly fishermen have long understood this relationship, fashioning their style of angling around this knowledge.

In many parts of the angling world, timetables giving the site and approximate time of the emergence of a well-known mayfly have been available for a number of years. The streams of the Smokies, however, are not dominated by any particular insect species or order, much the same as the mountainside flora is not dominated by any particular plant.

Aquatic insect populations are low in most cases. These streams are poor producers of food, primarily due to the acidic composition. Acid water is low in nutrients that are necessary in order for large concentrations of insects to exist. Other problems local insects must endure are acid rain and flash floods that scour the bottom of fragile life.

Just about every sort of mayfly that occurs in the Appalachians is found in the Park. However, the population densities of the aquatic insects are low, usually so low that even during peak emergence they play only a minor part in the trout's feeding habits.

Work done in researching the caddis flies of the Smokies, by several noted entomologists, reveals that the Tennessee Valley has one of the world's richest concentrations of caddis flies in the world. There are over 50 genera of caddis flies found in the Smokies, according to Dr. David Etnier, professor of zoology at the University of Tennessee.

Stone flies also do well in the swift pollution-free waters of the Park. The oxygen-rich cascading streams habor stone-fly nymphs, important to the trout's diet during certain times of the year.

Watch the surface of the water carefully if you plan to attempt to match the hatch. Hatches of mayflies can be found on almost any day from January through October. During the cold months, hatches usually occur during the warmest hours of the afternoon. Later, during mid-spring,

Big terrestrial fly patterns are recommended for late summer. Photo by Joann Kirk.

emergences can occur during mid-morning through late afternoon. By late spring hatches will be encountered in early morning and then in late afternoon. Summer is a time of limited, often sporadic insect activity. Activity is often limited to very early mornings and dusk. Matching the hatch is sometimes effective; however, presentation to these opportunistic feeders is really the key.

Traditional flies such as the Royal Coachman, Adams, Ginger Quill, and the Black Gnat found their way into the fly boxes of local anglers. Probably the most famous fly to come out of the Smokies was the Yallarhammar. There are numerous variations of this fly today on both sides of the mountains. It is basically a peacock herl-bodied wet fly, hackled with a split section of wing feather from a Yellow Shafted woodpecker, known locally as a Yallarhammar. It is illegal to kill this bird or sell flies using its plumage. However, the use of this fly is incredibly widespread, though its effectiveness is, in my opinion, no better than several other flies I could name. Other regional favorites include the Ramsey (it closely resembles a standard brown hackle), My Pet, Forky Tail Nymph, the nationally known Tellico Nymph, the Grey Hackle Yellow, Cotton Top, and the Thunderhead. The Thunderhead is a Wulff-style dry hairwing fly.

Well-known flies such as the Adams, Coachman, Kings River Caddis, and several other established patterns are also used with great success inside the Park. A dry fly that closely resembles a hair wing Adams, the Thunderhead, is the creation of Joe Hall, of Bryson City. Hall is perhaps the dean of Smoky Mountains fly tiers whose clients have included such well-known anglers as Joe Brooks. Frank Young, another Carolina trout fly tier, added one of the most interesting modifications to this fly I have ever seen. Young substituted the soft belly fur from a 'possum in place of the kip tail usually used in making the Thunderhead. The result is equally interesting as the fluffy 'possum fibers give the fly an added touch of drift as they fall gently on the surface of the water. The addition of the 'possum hair makes this an all-hillbilly candidate.

My Pet, the Ugly Devil, the Quill Tail, and Near Nuff are all of Western Carolina origins. The Grey Hackle Yellow, a delicate dry fly, is said to be the top choice of a number of Cherokee anglers.

The Streaker Nymph is another fly of Carolina origin. It is very similar to the Tellico Nymph, but more slender and lighter in color. A favorite of many Hazel Creek regulars, it is tied to mock the abundant stickbait found in the creek's flow.

Southern trout flies are beginning to become known nationally, as visiting anglers take these patterns home. Traditional patterns will take

Streamer patterns commonly used on Smoky Mountains trout. Photo by Joann Kirk.

An angler selecting a fly.
Photo by Don Kirk.

fish equally well. I know one top-flight dry fly fisherman who uses a #14 Royal Coachman exclusively. Table 1 provides a list of proven fly patterns and when they are most effective.

Table 1: Proven Fly Patterns

Fly patterns	Sizes	Dates effective
DRY FLIES		
Ramsey or Brown Hackle	#10–14	All year
Kings River Caddis	#10–18	April through June
Buck Caddis	#12–16	April through June
Red Quill	#12–16	May through June
Light Quill	#10–22	Late May through October
Joe's Hopper	# 8–12	June through October
Bee	#10–18	April through October
Japanese Beetle	#12	June through mid-August
Little River Ant	#12–18	June through October
Black Gnat	#10–18	All year
Irresistible	#10–16	All year
Near Nuff	#12–16	May through June

Table 1, continued

Fly patterns	Sizes	Dates effective
Grey Hackle Yellow	#10–18	May through July
Green Spinner	#10–16	April
Ellison's Greenbriar Series	#12–18	March–June
Male Adams	#12–18	April–June
Thunderhead	#12–18	April–June
Elkwing Caddis (brown or blonde)	#12–20	All year
WET FLIES		
Leadwing Coachman	# 8–16	All season
Yallarhammar	# 8–14	All season
Blue Dun	#12–16	April
Black Gnat	#12–18	Mid-May through August
Quill Gordon	#10–16	March through April
Squash Bug	#12–16	June through July
NYMPHS		
Tellico Nymph	# 8–18	April through mid-June
My Pet	#10–14	April through May
May Stone-fly Nymph	# 6–10	March through June
Streaker Nymph	#10–16	April through June
Cotton Top	#10–16	May through June
George Nymph	#10–16	All year
Stickbait	# 8–10	All year
March Brown	#10–16	October through May
Gold Ribbed Hares Ear	#10–16	All year
Light Cahill	#10–18	October through May
Solomon's Caddis Pupa	# 6–10	Late April through June
Stone-fly Nymph	# 6–10	September through mid-May
Montana Nymph	# 6–10	September through mid-May
Swannundaze Stone-fly Nymph	# 6–12	September through mid-May
Ugly Devil	#10	May through June
STREAMERS		
Black Nose Dace	# 6–12	
Muddlers Minnow	# 6–10	
Grey Ghost	# 6–10	
Little Rainbow Trout	#10	
Spudler	# 6–10	

Bases of Operations

Of the 8 to 9 million people who annually visit the Great Smoky Mountains National Park, approximately 40 percent enter the Park by way of Gatlinburg, approximately 23 percent by way of Cherokee, and approximately 15 percent by Townsend. Most stay in or near these locales and at Fontana Village Resort on the south shore of Fontana Lake. There are streams within minutes of each of the four major tourist stops.

GATLINBURG: The West Prong of the Little Pigeon River flows through the heart of the busy resort center. It offers excellent rainbow and brown trout fishing. Greenbriar River (the Middle Prong of the Little Pigeon River) is located six miles east of Gatlinburg off TN 73. This beautiful rivulet offers mediocre fishing for rainbow and brown trout also. Little River, located six miles from Gatlinburg by way of the Little River Road (former TN 73), offers good rainbow and brown trout fishing. Abrams Creek, one of the better streams in the Park, is easily accessible from the Cades Cove area, located 30 miles from Gatlinburg.

CHEROKEE: The Oconaluftee River and Raven Fork flow together just upstream from this picturesque town. Both of these fine streams offer very good fishing. The Transmountain Highway (formerly US 441) follows alongside the Oconaluftee, offering excellent access. Raven Fork is accessible upstream from the Park boundary by trail only. Deep Creek, which flows out of the Park near Bryson City, is also a sound bet for a day of good fishing.

FONTANA: Anglers wishing to sample the streams that flow into beautiful Fontana Lake can find no better base of operations than the Fontana Village Resort. Eagle, Hazel, Forney, and Chambers Creeks all flow into Fontana Lake. The resort's marina will rent boats to cross the lake or caddy anglers across to these streams and pick them up later for a modest fee. The lake offers superb smallmouth, walleye, and muskey fishing. More information is available from the Fontana Village Resort, P.O. Box 68, Fontana Dam, NC 28733.

The Gatlinburg, Cherokee, and Townsend entrances to the Great Smoky Mountains National Park account for anywhere from 70 to 80 percent of the annual traffic. There are other areas, which though less well known, can be equally sound choices.

COSBY: This entrance is popular, particularly among campers. From here you have excellent fishing opportunities at the nearby Greenbrier River (Middle Prong of the Little Pigeon River), the West Prong of the Little Pigeon (near Gatlinburg), Big Creek (off I-40 in North Carolina), and, of course, Little Cosby Creek at the campground.

BIG CREEK CAMPGROUND: Anglers staying here are among the most isolated in that the waters outside the Big Creek drainage are a considerable distance away. The nearest are the Greenbrier River (the Middle Prong of the Little Pigeon in Tennessee), and the Cataloochee Creek in North Carolina.

CATALOOCHEE CREEK: Campers/anglers here are in much the same shape as those staying at the primitive campground at Big Creek. Big Creek is the only other trout stream within a reasonable driving distance of Cataloochee Creek.

BRYSON CITY: This town makes one of the finest trout fishing bases on the North Carolina side of the Park. Deep Creek is only minutes from the Bryson City limits, and Noland Creek is only a short drive away on North Shore Road. The Oconaluftee River is also nearby.

ABRAMS CREEK CAMPGROUND: This primitive campground makes an excellent base of operations for fishing not only the lower portion of Abrams and its tributary, Panther Creek, but also nearby Twenty Mile Creek and Eagle Creek, plus a number of smaller streams such as Tabcat Creek, North Carolina.

An angler fishing Little River. Photo by Don Kirk.

Little River System

Little River

SIZE: large

FISHING PRESSURE: heavy

FISHING QUALITY: good

ACCESS: auto access available along the entire length of the stream in the Park

USGS QUADS: Wear Cove, TN

Little River was the site of early pioneer settlements and the hub of the largest logging operation ever carried out in the Smokies. The Little River Logging Company began cutting operations in 1901, which removed virtually every standing piece of timber by 1938. Those were wild times because with the logging came a thing seldom seen in the Smokies—hard cash. Logging camps were the sites of numerous duels and a place where moonshine flowed free. The scars from this mammoth cutting are evident even today, although the slopes are slowly recovering their lost splendor.

All three species of trout now reproducing in the Park can be found in the Little River system. The Park's largest known brown trout, a hefty 16 pounder, was taken from the East Prong in 1979. Large brown trout in the three- to seven-pound range are regularly taken from the deep pools of Little River throughout the year. Yet despite the fact that trophy browns are often taken, rainbow trout are the most abundant. Three- to four-pound 'bows are occasionally caught, particularly during the early spring and late autumn, but the average rainbow will be 7 to 9 inches long. While brook trout can still be found in this system, the brookie water was closed to all fishing in 1975.

Fishing is good on Little River and its numerous feeder rivulets. Fly fishermen can expect to find sporadic hatches of mayflies and caddis flies and hatches of large stone flies occur in April and May. Large browns are often taken on a well-tied stone-fly nymph.

Hardware fishermen will find themselves quite at home casting into the gin-clear waters of Little River. Lures such as Mepps spinners account for more trophy trout than any other angling method employed in the Smokies.

Anglers should note that during the warm summer months, the mainstream and the East Prong of Little River become crowded with fun-seeking swimmers enjoying the stream's cool waters. Fishing becomes nearly impossible when such activity reaches its mid-afternoon peak. The best angling during this time of year is in the early morning and late evening.

A quick look at a map of the Smokies reveals the Little River system is one of the largest in the Smokies, bounded to the south by Stateline Ridge, to the east by Sugarland Mountains, and to the west by Anthony Ridge. There are numerous other ridges and spurs that cut through the Little River Basin. The mainstream of Little River is formed by three primary tributaries: the East Prong, the Middle Prong, and the West Prong. All three feeder streams have their own well-developed tributary networks that deserve the investigation of adventurous anglers.

A rare, very large brown trout. Photo by Don Kirk.

East Prong of Little River

SIZE: large

FISHING PRESSURE: heavy

FISHING QUALITY: very good, particularly for brown trout

ACCESS: accessible by auto downstream from the Elkmont Campground to the Park boundary (13 miles) via the Little River Road (formerly TN 73); all other access limited to trail use

USGS QUADS: Clingmans Dome, NC-TN; Wear Cove, TN; Silers Bald, NC-TN; Gatlinburg, TN

The East Prong of Little River is often referred to simply as "Little River" by local anglers and National Park literature. Boulders the size of cabins are scattered along its course, plus an abundance of deep pools and long swift runs. Several of these spots have romantic names the local anglers use to enhance the tales of a day's fishin': The Sinks, Metcalf Bottoms, the Junction Pool, and the Little River Gorge are all spots Tennessee trout fishermen known by heart. Other spots known only to local anglers are such places as Ole Elmo's Hole and Widow's Pool.

One of the most heavily fished streams in the Park, the trout here are often selective, and a close inspection of your #12 Coachman by an 18 incher will certainly put an extra shot of adrenaline into your system.

Mayfly and caddis fly hatches are sporadic and often short lived. Very few hatches in the Smokies compare with those of the East, though occasionally a lucky angler will stumble upon a surprisingly heavy emergence that entices the trout to feast.

Upstream from the Elkmont Campground, Little River's character changes from that of a small river to a wild, cascading mountain stream. Fast pocket water, plunge pools, and beautiful scenery best describe this section. Beginning beneath Clingmans Dome, at an elevation of over 5,000 feet, Little River quickly picks up water from other brooks as it rushes down the steep slope. Brook trout prosper in many tributaries (most were closed to all fishing in 1975). Over 29 prongs of Little River begin at over 4,600 feet, with 15 beginning at over 5,000 feet. This is a diverse system with approximately 50 feeder streams draining its basin.

Access to East Prong of Little River

Little River is easily reached. Upstream from its confluence with the West Prong, for a distance of 14.5 miles, the stream is followed by the Little River Road, which winds alongside to its junction with the Elkmont Road. Upstream from that point, the Elkmont Road follows the river 1.5 miles to a point just downstream from the Elkmont Campground, a developed area with 340 campsites. The Little River Truck Road is open to autos for a distance of 1.5 miles.

Additional access to Little River is provided by the Little River Truck Road Trail, which begins at the end of the Little River Truck Road and follows upstream. At 2.8 miles the trail arrives at the mouth of Huskey Branch, a speckle trout stream. At 3 miles the trail arrives at the junction of the Cucumber Gap Trail. The Little River Truck Road Trail terminates at 4.2 miles at the confluence of Little River and Fish Camp Prong. Access to the mainstream is by the Rough Creek Trail, which begins at the end of the Little River Truck Road Trail. The Rough Creek Trail arrives at the junction of Rough Creek and Little River at 4.7 miles (from the terminus of the Little River Truck Road). At this point the Rough Creek Trail leaves the mainstream to continue on alongside Rough Creek. The Rough Creek backcountry campsite (N.P.S. #24, capacity 14) is located near the junction of the two streams.

Farther upstream, access to Little River is offered by a maintained trail most commonly referred to as the "Three Forks Trail." It begins at the junction of Rough Creek and Little River and follows the mainstream to 7.4 miles (from the terminus of the Little River Truck Road). The Three Forks backcountry campsite (N.P.S. #30, capacity 12) is located near this point. Grouse Creek flows into the mainstream near the campsite; it is a fine brook trout stream.

An old unmaintained path continues upstream alongside Little River (now only a small rill) to 7.9 miles, where the trail then leaves the mainstream to continue on alongside Kuwahi Branch (8.4 miles) before ascending Stateline Ridge.

Jake's Creek

SIZE: small
FISHING PRESSURE: moderate to light
FISHING QUALITY: fair
ACCESS: near Elkmont Campground
USGS QUADS: Gatlinburg, TN

Jake's Creek, a fairly good rainbow stream, flows into the mainstream 200 yards downstream from the Stone bridge at the upper end of the Elkmont Campground. It is reached by auto along the Jake's Creek Road from the Elkmont Summer Colony, upstream to .4 mile, the trailhead of the Jake's Creek Trail; the trail provides additional access to the stream for another 3 miles.

Fish Camp Prong

SIZE: moderately small
FISHING PRESSURE: closed 1975, upstream from the 3,240-foot-elevation trail crossing
FISHING QUALITY: good
ACCESS: Little River Truck Road
USGS QUADS: Silers Bald, NC-TN

Fish Camp Prong flows into the mainstream 4.2 miles upstream from the terminus of the Little River Truck Road. Fish Camp Prong and its tributaries, Goshen Prong and Buckeye Prong, are noted brook trout streams. Access is provided by the Fish Camp Prong Trail, which begins near the mouth of Fish Camp Prong. At 3 miles the trail arrives at the Camp Rock backcountry campsite (N.P.S. #23, capacity 8). A short distance from the campsite, Goshen Prong flows into the mainstream, reached from Goshen Prong Trail, which begins near the mouth of the stream and continues for 4.7 miles, before leaving the stream to ascend Stateline Ridge. The Fish Camp Prong Trail continues alongside the mainstream 4.3 miles to the junction of Buckeye Gap Prong. The Lower Buckeye Gap backcountry campsite (N.P.S. #25, capacity 8), a very nice fishing camp located above 3,500 feet amidst a beautiful forest of hemlocks, makes a wonderful spot to fry a meal of trout. There is no access farther upstream to the mainstream of Fish Camp Prong. The Buckeye Gap Trail begins here and follows tumbling Buckeye Gap Prong 1.5 miles to the stream's headwaters, before climbing Stateline Ridge. Note: This is an unmaintained path.

Rough Creek

SIZE: small
FISHING PRESSURE: moderate
FISHING QUALITY: good
ACCESS: Little River Truck Road
USGS QUADS: Clingmans Dome, NC-TN; Silers Bald, NC-TN

Rough Creek, which flows into the mainstream of Little River 4.3 miles upstream from the trailhead of the Little River Truck Road Trail, sports a combined population of rainbow and brook trout. It is reached via the Rough Creek Trail, which begins at the junction of Little River and Fish Camp Prong, and travels upstream .5 mile to the mouth of Rough Creek. The trail then follows Rough Creek 2 miles before leaving the stream.

Middle Prong of Little River

SIZE: medium

FISHING PRESSURE: moderately heavy

FISHING QUALITY: very good; the lower reaches have yielded some impressive brown trout in recent years

ACCESS: accessible by auto from its mouth (located .2 mile from the Townsend "Y") by the Tremont Road for a distance of 5.4 miles

USGS QUADS: Thunderhead, NC-TN; Silers Bald, NC-TN; Wear Cove, TN

Seasoned Smokies anglers refer to the Middle Prong of Little River as "Tremont." It has the reputation of producing some of the largest brown trout in the Park. A mammoth 12.5 pounder was wrestled from its shallow waters in July of 1980. Rainbow trout are predominate, though brook trout can still be found flourishing in the headwaters.

The confluence of Lynn Camp Prong and Thunderhead Prong mark the starting point of Middle Prong. Other key tributaries include Spruce Flats Branch and Indian Flats Prong.

Access to Middle Prong of Little River

Middle Prong is accessible to autos upstream from the mouth along the Tremont Road, located .2 mile from the Townsend "Y" on the Cades Cove Road (also known as the Laurel Creek Road).

The Tremont Road follows the stream, and at 2 miles the paved road ends and a gravel road (open to traffic during the fishing season) continues alongside the stream. At 3.5 miles Spruce Flats Branch enters the mainstream.

Spruce Flats Branch

SIZE: small

FISHING PRESSURE: moderate

FISHING QUALITY: fair

ACCESS: located 3.5 miles up from the mouth of Middle Prong

USGS QUADS: Wear Cove, TN

Spruce Flats Branch flows into the mainstream of the Middle Prong 3.5 miles upstream from the mouth of the Middle Prong. It is a small stream, often difficult to fish, and receives a moderate amount of fishing pressure, particularly near its junction with the mainstream. It is accessible via the Spruce Flats Trail, which begins near the mouth of the stream and continues upstream, offering good access to the headwaters.

Thunderhead Prong

SIZE: small
FISHING PRESSURE: fair
FISHING QUALITY: fair to good
ACCESS: Defeat Ridge Trail
USGS QUADS: Thunderhead Mt., NC-TN

Thunderhead Prong flows from the slopes of Thunderhead Mountain. The stream sports a mixed population of brook and rainbow trout. Sams Creek, a nice tributary of Thunderhead Prong, offers excellent fishing to those seeking an escape from the crowds. The Defeat Ridge Trail begins at the mouth of Thunderhead Prong and follows the stream. At .5 mile the trail reaches the mouth of Sams Creek, and at 2.3 miles leaves the stream for the last time to ascend the ridge.

Lynn Camp Prong

SIZE: small
FISHING PRESSURE: moderate (CLOSED upstream from junction with Indian Flats Prong)
FISHING QUALITY: good
ACCESS: excellent, Davis Ridge Trail
USGS QUADS: Thunderhead Mt., NC-TN; Silers Bald, NC-TN

Lynn Camp Prong is a fine little trout stream with an impressive tributary network. It boasts both rainbow and brook trout, though they are seldom over 12 inches long. Tributaries of Lynn Camp Prong include Panther Creek, a nice rippling stream, and Indian Flats Prong, an isolated rivulet. The Davis Ridge Trail follows Lynn Camp Prong from its mouth, reaching the mouth of Panther Creek at 2.5 miles. The trail provides access to Panther Creek 1 mile upstream before leaving the creek to climb Timber Ridge.

The Davis Ridge Trail continues upstream alongside Lynn Camp Prong and at 3 miles reaches the confluence of Indian Flats Prong. The Davis Ridge Trail (also known as the Indian Flats Trail) continues alongside beautiful Indian Flats Prong, which offers worthwhile fishing. At 4.7 miles the trail crosses the stream for the last time before ascending Davis Ridge.

West Prong of Little River

SIZE: medium

FISHING PRESSURE: moderately light

FISHING QUALITY: good

ACCESS: auto access to West Prong provided upstream from the stream's junction with the East Prong via the Cades Cove Road. It travels alongside the stream 2 miles. Laurel Creek, a tributary of the West Prong, continues along route an additional 4 miles

USGS QUADS: Wear cove, TN; Cades Cove, NC-TN; Thunderhead Mt., NC-TN

Most anglers who fish the Smokies overlook the West Prong of Little River, yet the stream offers good trout fishing. The roadside portion of the West Prong and its tributary, Laurel Creek, receives the heaviest angling pressure, while the section that passes through the backcountry is relatively untouched. Most anglers bypass the West Prong in favor of more highly touted nearby streams such as Abrams Creek and Little River (the East Prong).

Rainbow trout have long dominated the mainstream. A limited population of specs does exist in a few headwater streams. The West Prong, the smallest of the three prongs that form Little River, is bounded by Defeat Ridge, Stateline Ridge, and Bote Mountain. Key tributaries include Laurel Creek and Bee Cove Creek.

Access to West Prong of Little River

The West Prong is accessible upstream from its mouth by auto via the Cades Cove Road (also known as the Laurel Creek Road), which follows alongside 2 miles until the stream leaves the road.

Backcountry access is provided by the West Prong Trail (the trailhead is located at the Tremont Center), which crosses a ridge and at 1.7 miles reaches the banks of the West Prong, where the West Prong backcountry campsite (N.P.S. #18, capacity 8) is located. This is the trail's only contact with the West Prong.

West Prong of the
Little Pigeon River System

West Prong of the Little Pigeon River

SIZE: large to medium
FISHING PRESSURE: moderate to surprisingly light
FISHING QUALITY: very good to excellent
ACCESS: Newfound Gap Road follows alongside the path of the stream
USGS QUADS: Mt. Leconte, NC-TN; Clingmans Dome, NC-TN;
    Gatlinburg, TN

The West Prong of the Little Pigeon River has traditionally been the general over-mountain route of travelers for centuries. Long before white men cast their shadows on these mountains, Indians traveled to and fro across the crest of the ridge alongside this stream. During the early 1830s the Cherokees built a toll road that ran along the same route as Road Prong (thus the branch gained its name). During the Civil War, both armies used the West Prong as a route through the rugged Smokies. Colonel Clingman, the military explorer of the Smokies, also used it as his route when ascending Clingmans Dome, once thought to be the highest point in the eastern United States.

The West Prong's watershed was thoroughly logged to the fir forest line. This area's farming and commerce were well developed. The forest has regained much of its lost stature, but open meadows crisscrossed with hand-layed stone fences can still be found.

The West Prong has one of the steepest descents of any stream in the Smokies, draining some of the highest mountains in the Appalachian Range. Upon leaving the Park the stream flows through the center of Gatlinburg, then on to Severville where it joins with the Little Pigeon River. Primary tributaries of the West Prong include Dudley Creek, Roaring Fork, LeConte Creek, Walker Creek, and Road Prong. The

34

confluence of Walker Creek and Road Prong is the beginning of the West Prong.

Anglers staying in Gatlinburg or Pigeon Forge will discover that the West Prong offers Smoky Mountain trout fishing with only a minimum amount of fuss. The quality of fishing is surprisingly good despite its almost urban location. This stream abounds with a large number of 7- to 9-inch fish. Yet I've had more fish in the 16- to 18-inch class buzz my flies here than anywhere else in the Park.

At one time there was a rearing station at what is now the Chimney Tops Picnic Grounds. The stream annually received thousands of rainbow trout. The rainbows have done exceptionally well, reaching three to four pounds with regularity. Brook trout can still be found in several of the headwater streams, notably Road Prong.

Brown trout have invaded the lower stretches of the West Prong in recent years. Trophy browns are occasionally taken, but rainbows are by far the most numerous. The West Prong can be a treacherous little creek to get around on. Plunge pools are surrounded by deceptively slick "gray backs" (the local name for the huge gray boulders that litter the Smokies). In addition the stream is often very swift and turbulent. Accordingly, some stretches seldom see one or two fishermen a week.

The author fishing the West Prong of the Little Pigeon River. Photo by Joann Kirk.

Joann Kirk, in one of her rare moments in front of the camera, fishing the West Prong of the Little Pigeon River. Photo by Don Kirk.

Access to West Prong

The West Prong of the Little Pigeon River is accessible by auto from the Newfound Gap Road, which runs alongside the stream to about 4,500 feet. This road connects Gatlinburg, Tennessee, with Cherokee, North Carolina. There is ample roadside parking along the entire route, though traffic may at times be extremely heavy.

There are no maintained trails that offer continuous access to the stream. The National Park Service has in recent years established a number of "Quiet Walkways" which lead to the stream. It is amazing how few anglers utilize these pathways. There are no backcountry primitive or developed campsites located within the bounds of the West Prong of the Little Pigeon watershed.

Dudley Creek

SIZE: small
FISHING PRESSURE: light
FISHING QUALITY: good to excellent

ACCESS: accessible at the Park boundary from TN 73, approximately 1.8
   miles east of Gatlinburg
USGS QUADS: Mt. LeConte, NC-TN

Dudley Creek is a super little trout stream located only a short drive from
Gatlinburg. This stream is fished only occasionally by visiting anglers,
probably because of its relatively small size and somewhat obscure
location. The stream has a plentiful population of rainbow trout in its
lower reaches; brook trout can still be found in the headwaters.

   Novice anglers may find this a difficult stream to fish because of the
dense flora. Laurel and rhododendron thickets shroud many fine pools
from the reach of all but the most experienced casters. These dense,
overgrown sections of Dudley Creek rarely see the fraudulent offerings of
the fisherman.

   Tributaries of Dudley Creek that warrant mention are Twin Creek and
Little Dudley Creek.

Access to Dudley Creek

   Auto access to Dudley Creek is possible via TN 73. The stream passes
out of the Park approximately 1.8 miles east of Gatlinburg and flows
alongside the highway. There are no maintained trails inside the Park, but
an old National Park Service fire road provides excellent access to the
stream for a short distance.

Roaring Fork

SIZE: small
FISHING PRESSURE: light to moderate
FISHING QUALITY: excellent
ACCESS: accessible from the Roaring Fork Motor Nature Trail
USGS QUADS: Mt. LeConte, NC-TN

Roaring Fork has long been one of my favorite streams in the Smokies. It
is located near the heart of Gatlinburg, yet despite this almost
cosmopolitan locale, offers excellent rainbow and brook trout fishing.

   Roaring Fork boasts the distinction of having the most drastic descent
of any stream its size in the eastern United States. This fact accounts for
the loud roar and almost continuous series of cascades and deep pools.
These oxygen-rich waters support a prolific population of stone flies. A
well-tied stone-fly nymph cast into its foaming pools will produce action.

   Indian Camp Branch and Surry Branch are tributaries that offer good
fishing.

Access to Roaring Fork

Roaring Fork is accessible by auto from the Roaring Fork Motor Nature Trail, a one-way road. It is popular to park at the end of this road and walk in to fish, thus avoiding the drive around the loop.

The Trillium Gap Trail offers further access to the stream. It begins at the Grotto Falls parking area. At 1.5 miles it crosses the stream and at 4.4 miles arrives at the headwaters of Surry Branch, a tributary of Roaring Fork.

LeConte Creek

SIZE: small
FISHING PRESSURE: moderate
FISHING QUALITY: fair
ACCESS: auto access possible via the Roaring Fork Motor Nature Trail
USGS QUADS: Mt. LeConte, NC-TN

LeConte Creek is located alongside one of the most popular foot and horse trails in the Smokies. This fact has not enhanced the fishing. Everywhere hikers seem to grow like mushrooms. It is a nice little stream to fish, though privacy is elusive.

Access to LeConte Creek

Auto access to LeConte Creek is provided by the Roaring Fork Motor Nature Trail, which follows alongside the stream.

Trail access is provided by the Rainbow Falls Trail, which begins off the Cherokee Orchard Road at 4.3 miles, and follows the stream 2 miles to Rainbow Falls. The fishing quality upstream from the falls is poor.

Road Prong

SIZE: small
FISHING PRESSURE: moderate
FISHING QUALITY: excellent
ACCESS: mouth of the stream is located 8.7 miles south of the Sugarlands Center, on the Newfound Gap Road
USGS QUADS: Mt. LeConte, NC-TN; Clingmans Dome, NC-TN

Road Prong is one of the better streams forming the headwaters of West Prong. Rainbow trout occupy the lower levels of the stream. The upper reaches hold a fine population of frisky "specs." A total of seven tributary prongs begin at an elevation of over 4,800 feet.

Road Prong passes through the lovely Beech Flats area, considered one of the prettiest sections of the Smokies. There are a number of cascades and pools that can be easily fished by even a novice trouter.

Access to Road Prong

The confluence of Road Prong and Walker Camp Prong is 8.7 miles south of the Sugarlands Center, on the Newfound Gap Road. There is no further auto access to the stream.

The Road Prong Trail offers access to the creek farther upstream. It follows alongside the stream for 3.1 miles to its headwaters.

Walker Camp Prong

SIZE: small to medium
FISHING PRESSURE: moderate
FISHING QUALITY: poor
ACCESS: majority of the stream follows alongside the Newfound Gap Road
USGS QUADS: Mt. LeConte, NC-TN; Clingmans Dome, NC-TN

The confluence of Walker Camp Prong and Road Prong marks the beginning of the West Prong, which seems to have all the necessary qualities of a good trout stream. Unfortunately, the fishing is below par for this watershed.

The headwaters of Walker Camp Prong flow over a formation of acid-bearing shale known as the "Anakeesta Formation." For eons Walker Camp Prong flowed over this formation, gradually leeching out and sealing the bulk of the exposed rock's acidic properties. The pH of Walker Camp Prong was always low, but the brook trout and other aquatic life forms found it bearable. When the National Park Service found it necessary to widen the Newfound Gap Road alongside the path of the stream, the Anakeesta Formation was unwittingly cut into. The stream was then exposed to this freshly unearthed acid source. To make a bad situation worse, the silty-slatey Anakeesta was crushed into gravel and used as the bed for the new pavement.

The aquatic life of this little stream has been damaged by this act and the effects will be felt for several lifetimes.

Rainbow trout can be taken in the mainstream and there is still a remnant population of brook trout in the headwaters of the mainstream, but overall fishing here is poor.

Alum Cave Creek, a tributary to Walker Camp Prong, offers mediocre angling for brook trout. It flows into the mainstream at a point old-timers call "Grassy Place," a favorite camping spot for mountaineer anglers during pre-Park days. Olin Watson, president of the Smoky Mountains Historical Society, related an amusing story of a fishing trip that took place here around 1910. It seems a group of men from the flatlands decided to spend a few weeks up the West Prong doing a little fishin' and huntin'. At that time "specs" were thick as gnats and could easily be caught at any time. One evening while the day's catch was frying, the jug of moonshine made a round or two around the fire. Now, 'shine often makes for some mighty tall talk, and that evening the subject turned to how many fish a man could eat. As the tale goes, one fellow ate around 80 specs before stopping. He managed to keep the fish down, but declined to join the rest of the angling party the next day!

Access to Walker Camp Prong

Walker Camp Prong begins 8.7 miles south of the Sugarland Center on the Newfound Gap Road. This road offers excellent access to the stream to approximately 4,500 feet elevation.

Alum Cave Creek flows into the mainstream 1.3 miles upstream from the confluence of Walker Camp Prong and Road Prong. Further access is possible via the Alum Cave Trail, which begins at the mouth of the stream.

Middle Prong of the
Little Pigeon River System

Middle Prong of the Little Pigeon River

SIZE: large at the park boundary, smaller upstream
FISHING PRESSURE: heavy
FISHING QUALITY: fair, at its best in early spring
ACCESS: approximately first 3 miles upstream from the Park boundary are
    accessible to autos, all other trail only
USGS QUADS: Mt. LeConte, NC-TN, Mt. Guyot, NC-TN

The Middle Prong of the Little Pigeon River (locally referred to as the Middle Prong or Greenbriar Creek) is one of the more rugged watersheds. Prior to becoming part of a national park, Greenbriar Cove was a sparsely populated, primitive area. The terrain displays an ancient face. Wisely, the National Park Service chose not to develop this area, slowly phasing out camping and auto access. Partially logged in the 1900s, the area is well known for its virgin stands of huge trees and giant cherry.

The Greenbriar Creek watershed is located in the northwest section of the Park. Mt. LeConte, one of the highest peaks in the eastern United States, bounds the watershed to the south, with Mt. Guyot to the east. The primary tributaries are Porter's Creek, Ramsey Prong, Buck Fork, Eagle Rock Prong, and Chapman Prong.

Greenbriar is a rough-and-tumble cascading creek, rushing over thousands of huge boulders, forming countless trout-holding pools. Getting to these trout requires a bit of work, due to the extreme ruggedness of the terrain. But a day of fishing here is a sure-fire remedy for insomnia.

Greenbriar Creek sports all three species of trout. Rainbows are the most abundant. Brown trout have established a foothold in the lower

The author fishing Greenbriar River. Photo by Joann Kirk.

reaches as a result of stockings outside the Park. Brook trout still florish in the majority of the headwater streams.

Greenbriar Creek is not a premium trout stream. This watershed has been traditionally prone to flash floods, which not only kill fish, but have a scouring effect on the bottom fauna.

Greenbriar Creek is at its best in early spring. There is a good population of stone flies in this watershed, so stone-fly imitations (basically nymphs) are always trout getters. Nice hatches of small gray mayflies take place in the last few weeks of April, making for pretty fair fly-fishing.

Access to Greenbriar Creek

Greenbriar Creek flows under TN 73, 6 miles east of Gatlinburg. Entrance to the Park is possible by turning onto the Greenbriar Road at the concrete bridge.

The Greenbriar Road allows auto stream access as far as the ranger station (.9 mile). This section of road is open the year round. During the fishing season, an additional 2.5 miles of gravel road alongside the stream is also open.

Further access to the mainstream is possible via the Ramsey Prong Road Trail, which begins at the end of the road. It generally follows the stream, ending at the junction of Ramsey Prong (1.7 miles). There is no further access to the mainstream.

Porter's Creek

SIZE: medium
FISHING PRESSURE: moderate
FISHING QUALITY: good
ACCESS: the mouth of the stream can be reached by Porter's Creek Road
USGS QUADS: LeConte, NC-TN; Mt. Guyot, NC-TN

Porter's Creek is gentle and easier going than the mainstream. It would be difficult to be disappointed by a fishless day on this sparkling rivulet. The streamside flora is most engrossing.

Porter's Creek is primarily a rainbow trout stream, although there are still a few brook trout in the most remote headwater areas. The mouth of the stream is located 3.2 miles upstream from the Park boundary. Porter's Creek flows off the steep slopes of Mt. LeConte. Its principal tributaries are False Gap Prong, Long Branch, and Cannon Creek. False Gap Prong is perhaps the best fishing of the three.

Access to Porter's Creek

Automobile access to Porter's Creek is possible using the Porter's Creek Road, which begins at the junction of Greenbriar Creek and Porter's Creek (Porter's Creek flows from the right). This gravel road follows upstream 1 mile to a large parking area.

The Porter's Creek Trail, which starts at the parking area, follows alongside the stream to its headwaters.

Ramsey Prong

SIZE: small
FISHING PRESSURE: moderately light
FISHING QUALITY: fair
ACCESS: mouth of the stream is located 1.5 miles from the parking areas
USGS QUADS: Mt. Guyot, NC-TN

The headwaters of this little stream begin at an elevation of around 6,200 feet. It's a nice little brook trout stream. The only drawback is the occasionally crowded trail conditions. Fishing above the cascades is poor, not worth the effort.

Access to Ramsey Prong

The Ramsey Cascades Trail provides access up to the cascades (2.5 miles). There are no maintained trails upstream from that point.

Buck Fork

SIZE: small
FISHING PRESSURE: moderate (closed)
FISHING QUALITY: good, particularly in late summer
ACCESS: remote
USGS QUADS: Mt. Guyot, NC-TN

Buck Fork is a brook trout stream. Eight of the stream's prongs begin at an elevation of over 5,000 feet. Fishing all day up this stream is like spending a day in Maine. Towering fir and spruce shade the sun's rays, as the crystal-clear creek tumbles over moss-encrusted boulders into foaming pools. The closure of this stream in 1975 was sorely felt.

Access to Buck Fork

The mouth of Buck Fork is located .7 miles from the terminus of the Ramsey Prong Road Trail. Note: It is rough going to the mouth of the stream.

Eagle Rock Creek

SIZE: small
FISHING PRESSURE: moderately light (presently closed)
FISHING QUALITY: good
ACCESS: remote
USGS QUADS: Mt. Guyot, NC-TN

Eagle Rock Creek was a favorite haunt of mountain men during the pre-Park era. It's a good brook trout stream. Nine feeder streams begin at an elevation of over 4,500 feet. Eagle Rock Creek flows into the mainstream from the right 1 mile upstream from the terminus of the Ramsey Road Trail. Note: There are no access trails.

Chapman Prong

SIZE: small
FISHING PRESSURE: moderately light
FISHING QUALITY: fairly good, at its best in late summer
ACCESS: remote
USGS QUADS: Mt. LeConte, NC-TN

The confluence of Chapman Prong and Lost Creek forms the starting point of the Middle Prong of the Little Pigeon River. Chapman Prong offers fairly good fishing for speckle trout. The trout here are small, but scrappy and very colorful.

Streams such as this are at their best on rainy days during the hot summer months. A shower starts trout to feeding. Ant patterns are lethal during such times.

Access to Chapman Prong

Chapman Prong is in one of the more remote sections of the Smokies. The stream's mouth is located 1.6 miles upstream from the terminus of the Ramsey Road Trail.

Big Creek System

Big Creek

SIZE: large
FISHING PRESSURE: moderate
FISHING QUALITY: fair
ACCESS: only a small section of stream accessible by auto
USGS QUADS: Waterville, NC-TN; Luftee Knob, NC-TN

Big Creek is without a doubt one of the most beautiful streams in the Smokies. I've found that even on fishless days it is hard to leave this stream unfulfilled. The stream cascades down the mountain over massive gray boulders forming deep plunge pools, slows momentarily, then rushes on to the next stop. An added attraction is the fascinating variety of moss and lichen one finds attached to scores of streamside boulders.

Big Creek is located in the northernmost section of the Smokies. It is bounded by Mt. Cammeree, Mt. Sterling, and Mt. Guyot and flows into the Pigeon River. Primary tributaries include Swallow Fork, Gunter Fork, Yellow Creek, and Deer Creek.

The Big Creek watershed was thoroughly logged between 1909 and 1918, but under the protection of the National Park Service the forest has regained much of its original beauty. Further development has been halted and some access and facilities have been curtailed in recent years. Despite these efforts, however, this is a popular area due to its proximity to I-40.

The quality of fishing on Big Creek does not quite match the scenery. Most of the fish are small (five to eight inches) because Big Creek is not an exceptionally fertile streem capable of maintaining a population of trophy-sized trout. Anglers should also note that the terrain surrounding

Big Creek is rugged, so getting about is strenuous and can be dangerous if care is not taken.

Access to Big Creek

Big Creek is accessible by auto, by way of I-40 at the Waterville exit (451). Cross the Pigeon River (locally referred to as the "Dead Pigeon") and turn left. The entrance to the Park is approximately 2 miles away. From the Park boundary a gravel road follows upstream progress .2 mile to the Big Creek Ranger Station. Note: The stream is located 100 to 200 yards from the road most of the time. This road continues on to the Big Creek Primitive Campground (.5 mile), the end of the auto trail.

The Big Creek Trail provides further access to the stream. It begins off the gravel road a few hundred feet from the campground and from that point follows alongside the stream, offering fair to good access to anglers. At 5.2 miles the trail reaches the junction of Swallow Fork and at 5.6 miles arrives at the Walnut Bottoms backcountry campsite (N.P.S. #37, capacity 20). Walnut Bottoms is a superb fishing camp located on a flat, tree-covered area. This site allows easy exploration of several feeder streams flowing into the mainstream nearby and is the only backcountry campsite in the Big Creek basin. Walnut Bottoms is also the end of the Big Creek Trail. The Yellow Creek Trail begins at Walnut Bottoms and runs alongside Big Creek. At 6.3 miles (from the Big Creek Campground) the Yellow Creek Trail arrives at the junction of Gunter Fork, the starting point of the Gunter Fork Trail. Old maps of the Smokies refer to Big Creek upstream from this point as Mt. Guyot Creek, a name infrequently used today.

At 9 miles the stream reaches the junction of Yellow Creek. There is no maintained trail access to the upper mainstream. Deer Creek flows into the mainstream at 9.6 miles.

Swallow Fork

SIZE: small
FISHING PRESSURE: moderate
FISHING QUALITY: fair, at its best in mid-summer
ACCESS: mouth of the stream is located 5.2 miles from the campground
USGS QUADS: Luftee Knob, NC-TN

Swallow Fork is the first significant tributary encountered while traveling up Big Creek. It flows into the mainstream 5.2 miles above the campground. This stream has a combination of rainbow and brook trout.

John Mack Creek and McGinty Creek, tributaries of Swallow Fork, offer good brook trout fishing. A total of seven prongs begin at an altitude of over 4,400 feet.

Swallow Fork is a lovely little stream, well known for its canopy of impressive hemlocks, plus scenic waterfalls that roar like never-ceasing lions.

Access to Swallow Fork

The Swallow Fork Trail begins near the mouth of the stream and follows upstream 2.5 miles before leaving the stream to ascend Pretty Hollow Gap.

Gunter Fork

SIZE: small
FISHING PRESSURE: light
FISHING QUALITY: fair
ACCESS: mouth of the stream is located 6.3 miles from the campground
USGS QUADS: Luftee Knob, NC-TN

Gunter Fork flows through some of the most beautiful forest in the Park, and could be termed by anglers as the perfect size trout stream because it's large enough to allow comfortable backcast room for the average fly fisherman and small enough to cross at will.

Gunter Fork sports both rainbow and brook trout in its numerous pools and little "pockets." Fishing on this stream reaches its peak during the last weeks of May.

Access to Gunter Fork

The Gunter Fork Trail provides good access to the stream, beginning at Walnut Bottoms and running concurrently with the Yellow Creek Trail .5 mile to the mouth of Gunter Fork, where it then turns upstream alongside Gunter Fork for 2 miles before parting company.

Yellow Creek

SIZE: small
FISHING PRESSURE: moderately light (closed)
FISHING QUALITY: good, the hot summer months are usually productive
ACCESS: mouth of the stream is located 9 miles from the campground
USGS QUADS: Luftee Knob, NC-TN

Before it was necessary to close Yellow Creek in 1975, due to the precarious status of the brook trout in the Park's waters, this was one of the most popular speckle trout streams in the Smokies.

The old mountain men of the Cosby area were extremely fond of crossing the mountains from Tennessee and descending alongside this stream with a cane pole and a can full of red worms. For these rural farmers late summer was the time to "make camp" in the mountains, sometimes for weeks, until their crops were ready for harvest. Nightly, great fish fries were held in which hundreds of speckle trout were consumed and jars of moonshine were passed around the fire. Those were the days.

Access to Yellow Creek

Yellow Creek is accessible at its confluence with Big Creek from the Yellow Creek Trail. There is no maintained trail that lends further access to the stream.

Deer Creek

SIZE: small
FISHING PRESSURE: light (closed)
FISHING QUALITY: fair
ACCESS: remote
USGS QUADS: Luftee Knob, NC-TN

Deer Creek is a remote brook trout stream. My only experience on this stream involved the meeting of a large black bear. I came face to face with the bruin as I haphazardly rounded a lush rhododendron bush. He was equally startled, but appeared to maintain better kidney control through the entire ordeal. Since that time I have stayed away from this productive little stream.

Access to Deer Creek

There are no trails to this stream; its mouth is located .6 mile upstream from the junction of Yellow Creek and Big Creek.

Cataloochee Creek System

Cataloochee Creek

SIZE: large
FISHING PRESSURE: moderate to light
FISHING QUALITY: excellent, particularly good early and late in the season
ACCESS: requires a long drive over a gravel road
USGS QUADS: Dellwood, NC; Cove Creek Gap, NC; Bunches Bald, NC;
  Luftee Knob, NC

The Cataloochee Valley lies in one of the most remote sections of the Great Smoky Mountains National Park and is often referred to as the "Forgotten Far East."

Located off the established tourist path, Cataloochee has limited facilities—a ranger station and primitive campground (28 sites, located alongside the stream)—but a well-developed trail system. The Cataloochee Primitive Campground makes an ideal base camp for anglers wishing to sample Cataloochee's smorgasbord of trout streams.

The Cataloochee system is more like the combination of four separate streams that converge within a relatively short distance within the cove. The mainstream flows seven to eight miles within the Park, before leaving to later empty into Walters Lake, an impoundment of the Pigeon River.

The mainstream of Cataloochee Creek and a number of its tributaries flow through open fields and dales, often laced by weathered gray split-rail fences, an ever present reminder of the sturdy farmers who toiled in this green cove. Many local streams are named after familes that once resided here. Reunions of old Cataloochee families, held here every August, unite four to five hundred former residents and their descendants, a human heritage that bonds these mountains to the present.

This pastoral stream is not nearly so rough-and-tumble as are the

50

majority of waterways in the Smokies. Anglers from upstate New York will feel quite at home here; the stream has a generous helping of long slick runs, perfect for floating a sparsely dressed dry fly. Once discovered, Cataloochee becomes a personal Mecca that provides an escape from the crowds and hurried life-style of the outside world.

The mainstream of Cataloochee Creek is populated by a mixture of rainbow and brown trout, with trophies of each occasionally taken. Terrestrials such as leaf hoppers (jassids), grasshoppers, and several other seeasonal land insects are extremely important to the diet of these trout, particularly where the stream flows past open fields. Once while fishing below the campground, I was lucky enough to be on the stream while one of the fields was being mowed. With every pass of the mowing tractor a wave of fleeing grasshoppers would spangle the surface of the creek. The Hip's Hopper I used accounted for over 50 creel-size trout (both rainbow and brown) within a two-hour period (all were released). I would never venture to this valley without an assortment of terrestrial imitations.

The Cataloochee basin is bounded by the Cataloochee Divide, Mt. Sterling Ridge, and the Balsam Mountains. Its key tributaries include Little Cataloochee Creek, Caldwell Fork, and Palmer Creek, all possessing well-developed tributary systems that deserve the attention of anglers.

Access to Cataloochee Creek

Getting to this remote area requires a long drive over a gravel road. Approaching from the west along I-40, take the Waterville exit (451) and cross the Pigeon River. Turn left at the end of the bridge and follow the paved road 2 miles to an intersecton. Here turn left onto a gravel road (formerly known as NC 284) and continue on to the Cataloochee Valley (approximately 23 miles).

Upon reaching the Valley the New Cataloochee Road follows alongside the stream for 3 miles, arriving at the campground. The confluence of Palmer Creek and Caldwell Fork is located a short distance upstream. The confluence of these streams marks the starting point of Cataloochee Creek.

Little Cataloochee Creek

SIZE: medium to small
FISHING PRESSURE: light
FISHING QUALITY: good
ACCESS: accessible by auto for a short distance upstream from its confluence with the mainstream
USGS QUADS: Cove Creek Gap, NC

Little Cataloochee Creek is a miniature version of the mainstream, not dominated by a long all-encompassing single creek, but rather the result of several small streams converging within a short distance to form a medium-sized trout stream. Little Cataloochee Creek's headwaters begin well above 5,000 feet on the steep slopes of Mt. Sterling. Rainbow trout are most common in the lower and mid-reaches of the stream, with brook trout still occupying the upper portions.

Tributaries of Little Cataloochee Creek of angling merit include Coggins Branch, Conrad Branch, and Andy Branch for rainbow trout and Correll Branch and Woody Branch for brook trout.

Access to Little Cataloochee Creek

Old NC 284 travels alongside Little Cataloochee Creek upstream from its confluence with the mainstream to .3 mile, where Correll Branch enters Little Cataloochee Creek. The road continues alongside Correll Branch to 3,600 feet before leaving the stream.

Trail access to the mainstream of Little Cataloochee Creek is available via the Little Cataloochee Creek Trail. To reach the trailhead, drive 4.5

An angler at dusk in the Smokies. Photo by Don Kirk.

miles past the interesection of Old NC 284 and the Cataloochee Road (in the direction of Mt. Sterling). At that point there is a sign that reads "Little Cataloochee Baptist Church 2 miles." This is the starting point of the Little Cataloochee Creek Trail, which, for the first 1.5 miles, travels through a lovely forest setting. At 1.5 miles the trail arrives at Little Cataloochee Creek (the only contact the trail has with the mainstream), then travels on past Little Cataloochee Creek, and at 2.2 miles arrives at Coggins Branch. The trail follows Coggins Branch 2.6 miles before leaving the stream to climb Noland Gap.

Caldwell Fork

SIZE: small

FISHING PRESSURE: moderate near the campground, farther upstream pressure decreases

FISHING QUALITY: fish are small but plentiful

ACCESS: no auto access upstream from the mouth of the stream, which is located near the campground

USGS QUADS: Bunches Bald, NC; Dellwood, NC

The confluence of Caldwell Fork and Palmer Creek forms the starting point of Cataloochee Creek. Caldwell Fork is the smaller of the two streams, flowing off the Cataloochee Divide. It contains rainbow and brown trout in its lower reaches and a remnant population of "specs" in a few headwater areas. Over ten prongs of this stream begin at over 4,400 feet; however, the rainbow trout, the most abundant gamefish in the watershed, are the dominate species the entire length of the mainstream. McKee Branch, a small tributary, maintains a population of brookies.

Caldwell Fork receives a moderate amount of fishing pressure immediately upstream from the campground. The quality of fishing is good, but most fish are under creel size (five to eight inches).

Fishable tributaries of Caldwell Fork include McKee Branch, Big Bald Branch, and during the spring, Warm Cove Branch.

Access to Caldwell Fork

The Caldwell Fork Trail follows the mainstream from its confluence with Palmer Creek. The trailhead is located off the New Cataloochee Road near the mouth of the stream. Upstream at .8 mile, Den Branch flows into the mainstream, the starting point of the Booger Man Trail, a loop that rejoins the Caldwell Fork Trail at 2.5 miles near the confluence of Snake Branch.

McKee Branch is located at 3 miles and at 3.5 miles the trail arrives at the Caldwell Fork backcountry campsite (N.P.S. #41, capacity 10), located near a large open field known as the Deasening Fields. Anglers will find this section of stream particularly suited for the use of hopper flies during summer.

The trail continues upstream alongside Caldwell Fork. At 4.4 miles Double Gap Branch enters the mainstream. The Double Gap Trail offers access to Double Gap Branch, a very small branch of questionable fishing merit. Shortly after passing over Double Gap Branch the trail becomes known as the Big Poplar Trail. At 5 miles it leaves the stream for the last time to climb a small ridge, later terminating on the Rough Fork Trail.

Palmer Creek

SIZE: medium
FISHING PRESSURE: moderate to light
FISHING QUALITY: very good to excellent
ACCESS: accessible upstream by auto from the campground to the confluence of Rough Fork
USGS QUADS: Bunches Bald, NC; Luftee Knob, NC

The mainstream of Palmer Fork sports a mixture of rainbow and brook trout upstream from an elevation of 3,000 feet. Downstream from that point it holds rainbow trout and an occasional wayward brown. Palmer Creek offers anglers very good trout fishing on a number of very beautiful and productive feeder streams; Rough Fork, Pretty Hollow Creek, Lost Bottom Creek, Beech Creek, and Falling Rock Creek, all hold populations of brightly hued speckled trout. Each has its own little tributary system that can be a delight to explore.

The springs that form Palmer Creek, once known as Indian Creek, begin on the sides of the Balsam Mountains at an elevation of over 5,200 feet. From there the stream picks up a steady flow of water from feeder streams as it tumbles down. It passes through former grassy glades and old homesites before passing over the gentle terrain of the cove.

Access to Palmer Creek

The mainstream of Palmer Creek is accessible by auto for 1.6 miles upstream from the campground. Upstream from the confluence of Rough Fork the Palmer Creek Trail provides further access. The trailhead is located on the right side of Palmer Creek, 1.6 miles above the campground. It traces alongside the stream and at 1.5 miles Pretty Hollow Creek flows into the mainstream. This is also the site of the starting point for the Pretty Hollow Gap Trail (see Pretty Hollow Creek below).

The Palmer Creek Trail continues alongside the mainstream 2.6 miles, where Lost Bottom Creek enters. The confluence of Beech Creek and Falling Rock Creek is located at 3.1 miles. The combination of the two streams signals the beginning of Palmer Creek. The Palmer Creek Trail continues alongside Falling Rock Creek for a very short distance before leaving the stream.

Rough Fork

SIZE: small
FISHING PRESSURE: moderate
FISHING QUALITY: good
ACCESS: good, Rough Fork Trail
USGS QUADS: Bunches Bald, NC; Dellwood, NC; Cove Creek Gap, NC

Rough Fork flows into the mainstream near the Palmer Creek Trail starting point. Rough Creek, once known as "Ugly Creek," offers good fishing for rainbow trout. It is accessible upstream from its mouth via the Old Palmer Chapel Road. The road continues upstream alongside Rough Fork .9 mile where it terminates. The Rough Fork Trail lends additional upstream access to the stream. The trailhead is located at the end of the road. At 2 miles the trail arrives at the Big Hemlock backcountry campsite (N.P.S. #40, capacity 10), an excellent fishing camp. The trail continues upstream alongside Rough Fork only a short distance beyond the campsite.

Pretty Hollow Creek

SIZE: small
FISHING PRESSURE: moderate
FISHING QUALITY: good
ACCESS: Pretty Hollow Gap Trail
USGS QUADS: Luftee Knob, NC-TN

Pretty Hollow Creek flows into the mainstream 1.5 miles upstream from the trailhead of the Palmer Creek Trail. The Pretty Hollow Gap Trail follows the stream. The trail begins off the Palmer Creek Trail near the mouth of Pretty Hollow Creek, and at .2 mile arrives at the Pretty Hollow backcountry campsite (N.P.S. #39, capacity 20), also known as the Turkey George Horse Camp. The trail continues upstream alongside the stream to the 3-mile mark at which point it leaves the stream.

Oconaluftee River System

Oconaluftee River

SIZE: large

FISHING PRESSURE: moderately heavy to heavy

FISHING QUALITY: very good, lower reaches of the stream are noted for producing trophy brown trout

ACCESS: accessible upstream from the Park boundary by auto via the Newfound Gap Road (formerly US 441), which travels alongside the stream to its headwaters

USGS QUADS: Clingmans Dome, NC-TN; Mt. Guyot, NC-TN; Smokemont, NC-TN; Bunches Bald, NC; Luftee Knob, NC-TN

The Oconaluftee River is noted as a good brown trout stream. The stream is large, with an abundance of long, slow runs and deep pools. Browns exceeding 12 pounds have been wrestled from the crystalline waters of this river. Late fall is a favorite time for local anglers who employ a wide variety of large stone-fly nymphs to entice large browns. One fly I was shown, however, appeared to be an imitation of a large "tobacco worm." Constructed of raffia, the fly was dyed a deep green and tied on a #4 long-shanked hook. I attempted to trade for one of the odd-looking flies, but its owner, Jim Mills, one of Cherokee's most successful brown trout fishermen, told me that upon receiving this pattern from an old mountain man years before, he had promised to never give a copy of the fly to anyone.

Despite the presence of brown trout in the Oconaluftee River, the adaptable rainbows are the primary trout of the watershed. Their eagerness to eat almost anytime food appears makes them favorites with average anglers. Brook trout, too, still prosper in a large number of headwater streams, particularly in the raven Fork system.

56

The Oconaluftee River is deeply rooted in the human history of the Great Smoky Mountains. The Smokies were the cultural heart of the Cherokee Nation, whose domain once extended from the mountains of Northern Georgia throughout the entire Southern Appalachians. Prior to contact with the white man, the Cherokee civilization was considered to be the most advanced of any eastern North American Indians. Primarily farmers, their prowess in combat kept their neighbors in awe. The word *oconaluftee* in Cherokee means "by the river."

White settlers, attracted by the valley's fertile soil, first carved out homesteads in the 1790s. Later, during the mid-1830s, the federal government ordered the forced removal of all remaining Indians west of the Mississippi River. The result of this action upon the Cherokees has been named the "Trail of Tears." A small band of Cherokees, numbering around one thousand, refused to obey the order and retreated to the more remote sections of the Smokies. Later, the survivers of those who refused to leave were able to purchase the land that we now know as the Qualla Reservation.

The Oconaluftee River watershed is located in the center of the Smokies on the North Carolina side of the Park. The river proper is formed by the confluence of Beech Flats Prong anbd Kepart Prong. Other

The author fishing the Oconaluftee River. Photo by Joann Kirk.

key tributaries include Raven Fork, Mingus Creek (closed to all fishing), Collins Creek, and Bradley Fork. Raven Fork and Bradley Fork both have exceptionally well-developed tributary networks that are of considerable interest to anglers.

Access to Oconaluftee River

The Park section of the mainstream of the Oconaluftee River runs alongside the Newfound Gap Road (formerly US 441), for 10.4 miles to the junction of Kepart Prong and Beech Flats Prong.

Raven Fork

SIZE: medium
FISHING PRESSURE: local anglers use this stream on a fairly regular basis, but overall, does not receive a great deal of pressure.
FISHING QUALITY: good
ACCESS: remote
USGS QUADS: Smokemont, NC-TN; Mt. Guyot, NC-TN

Raven Fork is unique because it flows out of the Park, then comes back in. Its headwaters begin beneath the fir-lined ridges of Balsam Mountains and Stateline Ridge. A total of 11 prongs of Raven Fork's mainstream begin at an altitude of over 5,000 feet, with the majority of these feeder streams merging above 4,200 feet.

This is a rugged area, a fact which helped protect the streamshed from the wholesale logging that hurt many of the Smokies watersheds. Choice market trees, such as walnut and cherry, were selectively removed from the region, yet much of the valley remained intact.

The stream's native brook trout were possibly spared because, due to a combination of circumstances, including remoteness and fishing pressure, fewer than two thousand rainbow trout were stocked in Raven Fork. In contrast, the neighboring Oconaluftee River received over a quarter million rainbows. It has been theorized this has been a factor in explaining the population densities of the brook trout in the two adjacent streams. Raven Fork is one of the finest remaining brook trout waters in the Southern Appalachians. It was named in honor of "Kalanu," one of the Cherokee Nation's most revered war chiefs, who resided along the banks of this stream.

Raven Fork enters the Qualla Reservation near the Big Cove area, then near its confluence with the Oconaluftee River flows back into the Park. At the time of this writing the regulation of that portion of Raven Fork in the Park belongs to the Qualla Reservation. Directly upstream from the

The author fishing Raven Fork. Photo by Joann Kirk.

Qualla Reservation, Raven Fork flows through a section known as "the Gorge," which is considered to be one of the most rugged and primitive areas in the eastern United States. The water jets over weathered gray boulders, pausing in the depths of foaming pools before racing on. This section of stream offers very good fishing, but it should never be attempted alone.

Access to Raven Fork

The Park portion of Raven Fork is one of the most remote areas in the entire Smokies. To reach Raven Fork one must drive to the Cherokee Reservation. Big Cove Road, located off the Newfound Gap Road in Cherokee is the easiest approach route. Follow Big Cove Road, which travels along scenic Raven Fork, about 9 miles to the junction of Raven Fork and Straight Fork. Big Cove Road continues upstream along Raven Fork, and Round Bottom Road enters from the left leading up Straight Fork. Anglers wishing to follow Raven Fork should take Round Bottom Road, alongside Straight Fork, and at 1.2 miles pass through the Park boundary gate. At 2.5 miles Round Bottom Road arrives at the trailhead of the Enloe Creek Trail.

The trail offers the easiest access to the upstream sections of Raven Fork. It travels for a short distance along sparkling Hyatt Creek and at 2.7 miles arrives at the junction of the Raven Fork Trail. The Raven Fork Trail descends the ridge alongside the gushing waters of Enloe Creek to the banks of Raven Fork. Located at the junction of Enloe Creek and Raven Fork is the Enloe Creek backcountry campsite (N.P.S. #47, capacity 8), which is a super base camp for fishermen. It is nestled among some of the most spectacular cascades in the Smokies. Downstream from the campsite Raven Fork is accessible by a path that roughly follows the stream.

Upstream from the campsite the Raven Fork Trail winds along the swift waters of the stream. At 2.5 miles the trail reaches the abandoned Big Pool backcountry campsite. The Right, Middle, and Left prongs of Raven Fork all merge here forming a large, expansive pool, perfect for floating a dry fly. The trail leaves the stream to ascend Breakneck Ridge.

Straight Fork

SIZE: small
FISHING PRESSURE: light to moderate
FISHING QUALITY: good
ACCESS: near the Round Bottoms Picnic Grounds
USGS QUADS: Luftee Knob, NC-TN

Straight Fork offers good trout fishing opportunities to those seeking a nice stream with a limited road access. The stream holds both rainbow and brook trout. It is a decent-sized trout stream and fishing pressure is largely limited to local anglers. Round Bottom Road lends access to the stream, traveling 3.5 miles to the Round Bottom Picnic Grounds. There are no further maintained trails upstream from the picnic grounds. This is a tributary of Raven Fork which is a tributary of the Oconaluftee River.

Couches Creek

SIZE: small
FISHING PRESSURE: moderate
FISHING QUALIY: marginal
ACCESS: stream flows into the Oconaluftee River 5.2 miles upstream from the Park boundary
USGS QUADS: Smokemont, NC

Couches Creek is a small trout stream that is often overlooked for greener pastures elsewhere. It is picturesque, though scenery cannot entirely satisfy the desire to catch fish.

Bradley Fork

SIZE: large at its junction with the Oconaluftee, smaller a short distance
   upstream from that point
FISHING PRESSURE: heavy
FISHING QUALITY: excellent
ACCESS: accessible to anglers by an excellent trail system upstream from
   the Smokemont Campground
USGS QUADS: Smokemont, NC; Mt. Guyot, NC-TN

Many North Carolina trout fishermen feel Bradley Fork is one of the
better, if not the best, trout streams in the Smokies. It holds large brown
trout and colorful rainbow trout in abundance and sports an impressive
population of native speckle trout. Its size permits relatively easy casting
room for fly fishermen and spinner enthusiasts alike. The stream annually
produces mayfly hatches that capture the imagination of both anglers and
trout. The lower reaches of the mainstream are often crowded due to the
stream's reputation and proximity to the most popular campground in the
Smokies. Anglers willing to walk a couple of miles upstream will be
rewarded with relief from the crowds and better fishing.

Bradley Fork's feeder streams offer good fishing and are lovely. Among
these outstanding rivulets, all listed below, are Chasteen Creek, Taywa
Creek, Gulf Prong, and Chasm Prong. The mainstream of Bradley Fork
begins at the confluence of Gulf Prong and Chasm Prong. It is bounded
by the steep ridges of Richland Mountain and Hughes Ridge. Bradley
Fork empties into the Oconaluftee 6.5 miles upstream from the Park
boundary, near the Smokemont Campground. The Smokemont Campground has 180 campsites and is often crowded.

Access to Bradley Fork

Bradley Fork is accessible from its mouth to the upper end of the
Smokemont Campground by auto from the Smokemont Campground
Road. Upstream from the campground access is limited to horse and foot
travel.

The Bradley Fork Trail, one of the finest in the Smokies, follows the
stream to its headwaters. The trailhead is located at the end of the
Smokemont campground. At 1.2 miles you will find the confluence of
Chasteen Creek, also the site of the well-developed Lower Chasteen
backcountry campsite (N.P.S. #50, capacity 15), and the trailhead of the
Chasteen Creek Trail.

The Bradley Fork Trail continues on and at 4.1 miles arrives at the
junction of Taywa Creek, also the starting point of the Taywa Creek Trail.

At 4.3 miles the Bradley Fork trail passes the junction of Tennessee Branch, a fishable little feeder stream, and at 5.2 miles arrives at the Cablin Flats backcountry campsite (N.P.S. #49, capacity 20). It is a nice spot, though it can become very muddy during certain times of the year.

Upstream from the campsite the stream is reached via an unmaintained path, which continues upstream alongside the stream. At 6.3 miles is the confluence of Gulf and Chasm Prongs. At this point the path leaves the stream to ascend Balsam Ridge.

Chasteen Creek

SIZE: small
FISHING PRESSURE: moderately light
FISHING QUALITY: good
ACCESS: foot travel only, 1.2 miles from Smokemont Campground
USGS QUADS: Smokemont, NC-TN

Chasteen Creek flows into Bradley Fork 1.2 miles upstream from the Smokemont Campground. It offers good rainbow trout fishing. The Chasteen Creek Trail, which begins near the mouth of the stream, offers access to the stream. It runs alongside the creek and at 2.2 miles arrives at the Upper Chasteen backcountry campsite (N.P.S. #48, capacity 15). The trail continues on beside the creek for 3 miles before the stream becomes too small to fish.

Tawya Creek

SIZE: small
FISHING PRESSURE: light
FISHING QUALITY: fair to good
ACCESS: foot travel access only
USGS QUADS: Smokemont, NC-TN

Taywa Creek is the second significant feeder flowing into Bradley Fork upstream from the Smokemont Campground. The lower reaches of Taywa Creek hold brightly hued rainbow trout, while the headwaters are held by speckle trout. The creek is reached via the Taywa Creek Trail, which begins near the mouth of the stream, and follows alongside the stream for 1.5 miles.

Chasm Creek and Gulf Prong

SIZE: both are very small
FISHING PRESSURE: light
FISHING QUALITY: good
ACCESS: remote
USGS QUADS: Mt. Guyot, NC-TN

These two mountain rills merge to form the starting point of Bradley Fork. Both are primarily brook trout streams. The forest through which these aquatic gems flow is one of the loveliest in the Oconaluftee Valley. There are no maintained streamside trails offering access, but upstream progress via the streambed is usually possible.

Collins Creek

SIZE: small
FISHING PRESSURE: light
FISHING QUALITY: very good
ACCESS: stream flows into the Oconaluftee River 8.8 miles upstream from the Park boundary (at the Collins Creek Picnic Area); from the parking area an unmaintained trail lends further access
USGS QUADS: Smokemont, NC

Collins Creek is a surprising little mountain creek that offers very good fishing. I've never fished this stream without a nice fish taxing my tackle. I cannot say if this is an extraordinary stream or just a place where "lady luck" smiles on me.

An added bonus to fishing Collins Creek is the fact that it flows through a beautiful virgin forest upstream from the Newfound Gap Road. The lower reaches of the stream hold a mixture of rainbow and brook trout, while up in the headwaters brook hold dominion.

Access to Collins Creek

Collins Creek is reached at its mouth by auto from the Newfound Gap Road, 8.8 miles upstream from the Park boundary. Immediately upstream from its mouth Collins Creek passes through the Collins Creek Picnic Area. Beyond the picnic ground, access is limited to an unmaintained path, known as the Collins Creek Trail, for a distance of 2.6 miles.

Kephart Prong

SIZE: small
FISHING PRESSURE: moderately light
FISHING QUALITY: fair
ACCESS: merges with Beech Flat Prong alongside the Newfound Gap Road
   at 10.4 miles.
USGS QUADS: Smokemont, NC; Mt. Guyot, NC-TN

Kephart Prong was named in honor of Horace Kephart, the famous outdoor scribe of the Smokies. There was once a trout and bass rearing station located alongside this stream during the early years of the National Park. Today the stream offers anglers fair fishing for rainbows. The brookies have disappeared from this streamshed.

Access to Kephart Prong

Kephart Prong is accessible by auto at its mouth via the Newfound Gap Road, 10.4 miles upstream from the Park boundary. The Kephart Prong Trail offers additional access to the stream. Its trailhead is located near the mouth of the stream, off the highway. It follows upstream alongside Kephart Prong and at 2 miles arrives at the Kephart shelter (capacity 14). Here, the Kephart Prong Trail ends and the Grassy Branch Trail and the Sweet Heifer Creek Trail begin. Both offer further access to tributaries of Kephart Prong.

Beech Flats Prong

SIZE: small
FISHING PRESSURE: moderate to light
FISHING QUALITY: fair to somewhat poor
ACCESS: accessible by auto from the Newfound Gap Road for a short
   distance upstream from its confluence with Kephart Prong
USGS QUADS: Smokemont, NC; Mt. Guyot, NC-TN

Beech Flats Prong is, in truth, the upstream extension of the mainstream of the Oconaluftee River. It is a scenic little rivulet, though not a particularly outstanding trout stream. The stream flows over a formation of acid-bearing shale known as "Anakeesta Formation." For eons Beech Flat Prong flowed over this formation, gradually leeching out and sealing the bulk of the exposed "hot" rocks' acidic properties. The pH of Beech Flats Prong was always low, but the brook trout and other aquatic life forms found it bearable and prospered. When the National Park Service thought it necessary to widen the Newfound Gap Road alongside the path of the stream, the Anakeesta Formation was unwittingly cut into. The stream was then exposed to this freshly unearthed acid source. To make a bad situation worse, the silty-slatey Anakeesta was crushed into gravel and used as the bed for the new pavement.

The aquatic life of this little stream has been damaged by this act and the effects will be felt for several lifetimes.

Kanati Fork is a nice little tributary of Beech Flats Prong.

Access to Beech Flats Prong

The Newfound Gap Road follows alongside the route of Beech Flats Prong for 2.8 miles. Upstream from the highway's last contact with the stream, a National Park service road parallels the stream to its headwaters.

Kanati Fork

SIZE: very small
FISHING PRESSURE: light
FISHING QUALITY: very good
ACCESS: Kanati Fork Trail lends excellent access
USGS QUADS: Smokemont, NC-TN

Kanati Fork, a tributary of Beech Flats Prong, is a small stream often overlooked by anglers. It offers great fishing for native brook trout. *Kanati* is Cherokee meaning "lucky hunter." Anglers wishing to try their luck here should by all means employ the use of barbless hooks or crimp down the barbs of flies used. Kanati Fork is accessible by auto at its mouth via the Newfound Gap Road. It enters the mainstream 10.6 miles upstream from the Park boundary. The Kanati Fork Trail lends access to the stream beyond that point. Its trailhead is located near the mouth of the stream and provides fair access for a short distance.

Kanati Fork flows into Beech Flats Prong, the headwaters of the Oconaluftee River.

Deep Creek System

Deep Creek

SIZE: large

FISHING PRESSURE: moderately heavy near the campground, moderate in the backcountry

FISHING QUALITY: very good

ACCESS: auto access to the stream possible at the campground

USGS QUADS: Bryson City, NC; Clingmans Dome, NC-TN

Deep Creek is one of the more highly publicized streams in the Smokies. Trophy brown trout over ten pounds have been wrestled from its emerald-green pools. Few things can compare with a 16-inch rainbow emptying the line from your reel as it flees down one of Deep Creek's swift runs.

Brook trout still flourish in the headwater streams. You will begin to encounter these aquatic jewels at an elevation of approximately 3,600 feet. It is good to carry several fly patterns tied on barbless hooks, or pliers for crimping down the barbs on your flies when backcountry fishing here. A safely returned brook trout has an excellent chance of survival, whereas an injured "spec" might never recover from an encounter with a barbed hook.

This valley was spared some of the wholesale destruction loggers levied on the majority of the watersheds of the Smokies. Deep Creek's rough terrain made getting the lumber out uneconomical, although valuable species such as poplar, walnut, and cherry were selectively cut.

Deep Creek was the favorite haunt of Horace Kephart, the famous Bryson City resident and early advocate for the creation of a national park in the Southern Appalachian highlands. Kephart made many trips up this stream, recording his experiences in his writing. This was also the favorite fishing spot of the mountaineer fishing guide, Mark Cathey.

Cathey guided numerous parties into this valley and delighted in showing the elite anglers of the East his awesomely deadly "dance of the fly."

Deep Creek is fortunate to possess a rich aquatic insect community. Mayfly hatches are heaviest during the early spring and late summer. In addition, Deep Creek is noted for its large population of stone flies. The only drawback to fishing Deep Creek is the steady stream of tube-riding fun seekers who systematically filter down the last mile or so of the stream.

Deep Creek is bounded by Thomas Ridge, Stateline Ridge, and the Noland Divide. Its principal tributaries are Indian Creek, Bridge Creek, Pole Road Creek, the Left Fork, Nettle Branch, Cherry Creek, Rocky Fork, and Sahlee Creek.

Access to Deep Creek

Deep Creek has auto access from the Deep Creek Campground, located south of Cherokee via US 19 through Bryson City (from Bryson City the route is well marked). Access upstream from the campground is provided by the Deep Creek Road Trail. This auto trail begins at the campground and terminates at 2.2 miles at the trailhead of the Deep Creek Trail.

A native Great Smoky Mountains National Park trout caught and released in Deep Creek. Photo by Don Kirk.

The Deep Creek Hiking Trail follows intermittently alongside the stream and at 2.6 miles (from the Deep Creek Campground) arrives at the Bumgardener Branch backcountry campsite (N.P.S. #60, capacity 10). This is a small campsite, located 100 feet from the stream. At 5.3 miles is the McCracken Branch backcountry campsite (N.P.S. #59, capacity 6), a popular fishing camp. At 5.5 miles is the Nicks Nest Branch backcountry campsite (N.P.S. #58, capacity 6), and at 6.1 miles is the Bryson Place backcountry campsite (N.P.S. #57, capacity 20). The Burnt Spruce backcountry campsite (N.P.S. #56, capacity 10) is located .3 mile upstream from the Bryson Place site.

Pole Road Creek is located at 7 miles and is the site of the Pole Road backcountry campsite (N.P.S. #55, capacity 15), also the trailhead of the Pole Road Trail. At 7.4 miles the Left Fork of Deep Creek flows into the mainstream, and at 8 miles is the Nettle Creek backcountry campsite (N.P.S. #54, capacity 8), a popular streamside camp. Beetree Creek joins the mainstream at 8.4 miles, and at 10.4 miles the trail passes the Poke Patch backcountry campsite (N.P.S. #53, capacity 12). The confluence of Deep Creek and Rocky Fork is located at 11.6 miles, and at 12.5 miles is the junction of Sahlee Creek. The trail continues alongside the stream to 4,060 feet before ascending Thomas Ridge.

Indian Creek

SIZE: medium
FISHING PRESSURE: moderately heavy
FISHING QUALITY: good
ACCESS: mouth of the stream is located 2.2 miles from the campground
USGS QUADS: Bryson City, NC; Clingmans Dome, NC-TN

Indian Creek is a medium-size stream that offers good fishing. The headwaters of this stream lie tucked between the steep grades of Thomas Ridge and Sunkota Ridge.

Brown trout are occasionally landed in the extreme downstream portion of Indian Creek, though rainbows are the stream's dominate species. Brookies have all but vanished from the streamshed.

Indian Creek is a popular fishing spot and the trail leading to the stream is often crowded with sightseers who find the walk to Indian Falls irresistible.

Access to Indian Creek

The Indian Creek Trail provides access to the stream. It follows alongside the stream to the falls and at 4 miles leaves the stream. An unmaintained path provides further access to the stream.

A rare backwoods cabin near Indian Creek. Photo by Joann Kirk.

Pole Road Creek

SIZE: small
FISHING PRESSURE: moderate
FISHING QUALITY: very good
ACCESS: mouth of the stream is 7 miles from the campground
USGS QUADS: Bryson City, NC; Clingmans Dome, NC-TN

Pole Road Creek is a small but respectable trout stream. The trout population is composed primarily of rainbows, but a fragile community of brook trout can be found in the headwaters. The trout in this stream are surprisingly wary of anglers.

Access to Pole Road Creek

The Pole Road Trail provides access to Pole Road Creek. It begins at the mouth of the stream (which is located 7 miles upstream from the campground, after a ford of Deep Creek). The trail follows alongside the stream for 2 miles before leaving to ascend Sassafras Gap.

The Left Fork of Deep Creek

SIZE: medium
FISHING PRESSURE: moderate
FISHING QUALITY: very good, at its best from late spring through early fall
ACCESS: mouth of the stream is 7.4 miles upstream from the campground
USGS QUADS: Clingmans Dome, NC-TN

The Left Fork is one of the largest tributaries in the Deep Creek watershed. The mouth of the stream (.4 mile upstream from the Pole Road trailhead) is sometimes difficult to locate from the Deep Creek Trail. The best method for reaching this stream is to fish upstream from Pole Road Creek to the mouth.

The lower reaches of the stream are dominated by rainbow trout. The headwaters support a good population of brookies. Five prongs of this stream begin at an elevation of over 4,800 feet, and to most experienced southern trout fishermen, that spells "specs."

Noteworthy tributaries of the Left Fork are Bearpen Branch and Keg Drive Branch.

Access to the Left Fork of Deep Creek

There is an old unmaintained trail that follows the stream, but it is at times difficult to locate.

Beetree Creek

SIZE: small
FISHING PRESSURE: closed (moderate)
FISHING QUALITY: fair to poor
ACCESS: mouth of the stream is located 8.4 miles upstream from the campground
USGS QUADS: Clingmans Dome, NC-TN

Beetree Creek was once a productive brook trout stream. It is located in one of the loveliest coves in the Smokies. Massive poplars and hemlocks tower above the stream like eternal guardians. Unfortunately in recent years the quality of fishing on this stream has eroded, making it a poor choice.

Access to Beetree Creek

The stream has no access trails.

Rocky Fork

SIZE: small
FISHING PRESSURE: moderate to light
FISHING QUALITY: good
ACCESS: mouth of the stream is located 11.6 miles from the campground; however, anglers should note that distance from Newfound Gap is 2.8 miles
USGS QUADS: Clingmans Dome, NC-TN

Rocky Fork is a picturesque mountain brook. Tumbling cascades and cool, clear pools are an open invitation to fishermen. It has a combination of rainbow and brook trout at the mouth of the stream, but as one progresses upstream it quickly becomes a purely brook trout residence.

This is one of the better brook trout streams that was not closed in 1975, but anglers should be forewarned that this is a backcountry stream, located in a fairly remote section of the Park. When you decide to fish in such a place you must depend upon yourself. Should you be injured, it could be days, weeks, or even longer before another human casts a shadow on your face.

Access to Rocky Fork

The stream has no access trails.

Sahlee Creek

SIZE: small
FISHING PRESSURE: closed (moderate)
FISHING QUALITY: good
ACCESS: mouth of the stream is located 12.5 miles upstream from the campground; however, anglers should note that distance from Newfound Gap is 1.9 miles
USGS QUADS: Clingmans Dome, NC-TN

Sahlee Creek suffers from being too easily reached from Newfound Gap. Partially as a result of this the stream was closed to all fishing in 1975. A beautiful stream with an unusual number of dead-falls crisscrossing it, Sahlee Creek is a physically tiring stream to fish.

Access to Sahlee Creek

There are no streamside trails.

Noland Creek System

Noland Creek

SIZE: medium

FISHING PRESSURE: moderate near the mouth of the stream, somewhat less intense farther upstream

FISHING QUALITY: very good

ACCESS: reached by auto from the North Shore Road, by way of Bryson City; from there it is approximately 7 miles

USGS QUADS: Clingmans Dome, NC-TN; Bryson City, NC-TN; Noland Creek, NC; Silers Bald, NC-TN

The Noland Creek Valley seems to impart tranquility and peace of mind. Most of Noland's headwater streams flow through stands of virgin forest, making fishing here a delight.

The overpowering beauty of this valley has not been forgotten by its former residents. The area's rural dwellers were reluctant to leave their homes when the Park was created. Former landowners and their descendants frequently come here to fish and walk among the tall trees they refer to with misty eyes as the "old home place."

The Noland Creek watershed, during the pre-Park era, was a remote farming community. The families living here in the hollows and coves of the valley supported themselves raising corn and cattle. Corn not needed for bread or fed to the cattle during the winter usually found its way through the copper lining of a still. Making mountain corn "likker," or moonshine, was not only an honored art in the mountains of the South, but a reliable source of hard cash. During lean times, which were so common in this area, it often helped put shoes on the children.

At the turn of the century, the Noland Creek watershed was passed over by the logging operators who sprang upon the Smokies like hungry wolves upon the fold. There were selective cuttings of valuable market species, and clearing tillable ground, but most of the ridge lines are still covered with virgin growth.

Fishing on Noland Creek is very good. In recent years brown trout have established themselves in the lower sections of the mainstream. Spinner fishermen using such lures as a single hook Mepps Squirreltail spinner take occasional trophy browns from Noland Creek.

Rainbow trout are common from the mouth of the stream to about 4,000 feet, and they average 7 to 9 inches. But don't be too surprised by the surge of a 16 incher if you drop the right offering in the right spot at the right time.

Brook trout flourish in the headwaters of several streams. Anglers planning to fish the backcountry should make a point to bring along flies tied on barbless hooks, or pliers for crimping down barbs.

Noland Creek is located in the southeast section of the Great Smoky Mountains National Park. It is one of the smallest major streams flowing out of the Smokies into Fontana Lake. It is bounded by Forney Ridge, Stateline Ridge, and the Noland Divide. The principal tributaries of the mainstream include Bearpen Branch, Mill Creek, Bald Branch, Salola Branch, and Clingmans Creek.

Access to Noland Creek

Noland Creek flows into the Tuckasegee River Branch of Fontana Lake. It is accessible by auto from North Shore Road (which can be reached via US 19 through Bryson City), which crosses the Noland Divide and reaches the stream approximately 7 miles.

The Noland Creek Trail provides further stream access. The trailhead is located near the Noland Creek Bridge, off the highway. The trail travels alongside the stream and arrives at the confluence of Bearpen Branch and the Bearpen Branch backcountry campsite (N.P.S. #65, capacity 8) at approximately 1.7 miles. The trail continues upstream and at 4 miles reaches the junction of Mill Creek in the Salola Valley, the site of the Mill Creek Horse Camp backcountry campsite (N.P.S. #64, capacity 20) and the trailhead of the Springhouse Branch Trail.

At 6 miles the trail arrives at the Jerry Flat backcountry campsite (N.P.S. #63, capacity 10) and at 7.2 miles is located the Upper Ripshin backcountry campsite (N.P.S. #62, capacity 12). The trail continues upstream alongside Noland Creek until reaching the confluence of Sassafras Branch at 8.8 miles, before leaving Noland Creek to ascend the Noland Divide.

The Bald Creek backcountry campsite (N.P.S. #61, capacity 12) is located 200 yards upstream from the confluence of Sassafras Branch near the junction of Bald Branch and Noland Creek. Upstream from the Bald

Creek site the mainstream is accessible by an unmaintained path that closely follows the stream to the confluence of Salola Branch at 10 miles. Clingmans Creek flows into the mainstream at 10.8 miles.

Bearpen Branch

SIZE: small
FISHING PRESSURE: light
FISHING QUALITY: fair
ACCESS: mouth of the branch is located 1.7 miles upstream from the Noland Creek Trail starting point; no streamside trails
USGS QUADS: Noland Creek, NC

Bearpen Branch is purely a rainbow trout fishery. Fishing pressure on this small stream is light, despite its proximity to the North Shore Road. There are several unnamed tributaries that sport a few trout. Anglers should note that the terrain surrounding this little stream is very rugged.

Mill Creek

SIZE: small
FISHING PRESSURE: light
FISHING QUALITY: very good
ACCESS: remote
USGS QUADS: Clingmans Dome, NC-TN; Silers Bald, NC-TN

Mill Creek is one of the most important streams flowing into Noland Creek. It enters the mainstream in the lovely Salola Valley, which, during the pre-Park era, was a busy community and later the site of a ranger station.

The lower portion of the stream is dominated by rainbow trout, but the headwaters still contain a healthy community of speckle trout.

Springhouse Branch, a noteworthy tributary of Mill Creek, flows into the mainstream a short distance upstream from the Mill Creek Horse Campsite. It passes through a virgin forest and contains only rainbow trout.

Access to Mill Creek

The Springhouse Branch Trail offers limited access to Mill Creek and Springhouse Branch. It begins near the mouth of Mill Creek and travels alongside the stream. At .7 mile upstream the trail crosses Mill Creek and from that point continues up the Springhouse Branch. At 1.2 miles the trail leaves the stream to ascend Forney Ridge.

Bald Branch, Salola Branch, and Clingmans Creek

SIZE: all are small
FISHING PRESSURE: moderate (closed)
FISHING QUALITY: very good
ACCESS: remote
USGS QUADS: Clingmans Dome, NC-TN

These are some of the most popular brook trout streams in the Park. The ease of descending from Clingmans Dome has proved to be something less than a blessing. All three rivulets were closed to all fishing in 1975 to protect the brook trout stock.

Access to Bald Branch, Salola Branch, and Clingmans Creek

There are no maintained trails offering access to any of these streams. Bald Branch flows into the mainstream 9 miles upstream from Fontana Lake or 4.5 miles from the Clingmans Dome Road. Salola Branch flows into the mainstream 10 miles upstream from Fontana Lake or 3.5 miles from the Clingmans Dome Road. Clingmans Creek flows into the mainstream 10.8 miles upstream from Fontana Lake or 2.7 miles from the Clingmans Dome Road.

The author fishing for high-country speckle trout. Photo by Joann Kirk.

Forney Creek System

Forney Creek

SIZE: medium
FISHING PRESSURE: moderate to light
FISHING QUALITY: very good
ACCESS: all access limited to boat, foot travel, or horseback
USGS QUADS: Noland Creek, NC; Silers Bald, NC-TN

Forney Creek is well known to anyone who has spent time fishing in the Smokies, although it has not received the attention given several of the more highly publicized fishing spots. Its remote location, plus the fact it is situated between two of the most famous streams in the Park—Hazel Creek and Deep Creek—spares it from the burden of excessive angling pressure. Local anglers from Tennessee and North Carolina are often about the only folks you will encounter fishing this sparkling stream.

The Forney Creek watershed was one of the most thoroughly devastated valleys in the Great Smoky Mountains National Park. It was the site of an intensive logging operation that clear-cut the coves and slopes without mercy. A massive forest fire that occurred during the mid-twenties, fed by the slash left behind by the timbermen, consumed what remained of the valley's flora. As with many of the lumbered-out sections of the Smokies, this one has slowly regrown under the protective sanctions of the National Park Service, yet deep scars heal slowly. Hikers and fishermen should not depend on old maps of this valley since the devastation of the past altered many of the old trails.

The stream possesses an exceptional population of frisky, colorful rainbow trout. Each summer a number of trophy-size 'bows are taken from this stream, though the majority of fish caught will fall into the seven- to nine-inch range. (The Forney Creek outlet bay on Fontana Lake offers very good fishing for winter run spawning rainbows.)

Brook trout can still be found in the stream's upper reaches. They are a fragile remnant population that under no circumstances should be disturbed. Habitat destruction dating back to the logging era and competition with rainbow trout have placed the future of the brookie in this watershed in grave danger.

Forney Creek is located in the southeastern section of the Smokies. It is bounded by Forney Ridge, Stateline Ridge, and Welch Ridge and empties into Fontana Lake. Forney Creek has a well-developed network of tributaries including Bear Creek, Advalorem Branch, Bee Gum Branch, Slap Camp Branch, Whitemans Glory Creek, Jonas Creek, Huggins Creek, Little Steeltrap Creek, and Steeltrap Creek.

Access to Forney Creek

There is no auto access to this stream; you reach it via boat, foot travel, or horseback. It is popular to visit this watershed by horseback, which allows for fast travel and ease in carrying gear. Several of the backcountry campsites along Forney Creek accommodate horseback travelers.

Upstream from Fontana Lake, you'll find the Forney Creek Trail, which begins at the mouth of the stream. Located approximately 100 yards upstream is the lower Forney backcountry campsite (N.P.S. #74, capacity 12), an excellent fishing camp. At .6 mile upstream the trail arrives at the junction of Bear Branch and trailhead of the Jumpup Trail. The Bear Creek backcountry campsite (N.P.S. #73, capacity 15) lies west of the stream junction.

The junction of Forney Creek and Bee Gum Branch is located upstream 2.6 miles. This is also the location of the trailhead for the Bee Gum Branch Trail and nearby is the CCC Camp backcountry campsite (N.P.S. #71, capacity 12). At 3.3 miles the trail arrives at the junction of Slab Camp Branch, and at 4.1 miles is the junction of Jonas Creek. This is also the location of the trailhead of the Jonas Creek Trail and the Jonas Creek backcountry campsite (N.P.S. #70, capacity 12).

Huggins Creek flows into the mainstream 5.3 miles upstream. The Huggins backcountry campsite (N.P.S. #69, capacity 12), also referred to as the Monteith campsite, is located near the stream's fork. The Forney Creek Trail passes a sign 6.9 miles up indicating the direction of the Steeltrap backcountry campsite (N.P.S. #68, capacity 8). The trail crosses Little Steeltrap Creek at 7 miles, leaving the mainstream of Forney Creek to travel along the gentle slopes of Wild Cherry Ridge. Near 8.8 miles the trail fords Steeltrap Creek and resumes its streamside ascent of the ridge alongside Forney Creek. The trail continues to furnish excellent access to Forney Creek to about the 9.7-mile mark, where it then leaves Forney Creek for the last time to later terminate 1 mile from Clingmans Dome.

Bear Branch

SIZE: small
FISHING PRESSURE: light
FISHING QUALITY: fair
ACCESS: remote
USGS QUADS: Noland Creek, NC

Bear Branch is a small stream that offers fair fishing for streambound rainbow trout. It cannot be said this is the finest stream in the Forney Creek watershed. Most of the rainbow trout taken in this stream are below creel size (averaging five to seven inches in length).

Access to Bear Branch

Bear Branch is accessible upstream from its confluence with Forney Creek via the Jumpup Ridge Trail. The trailhead is located at the mouth of Bear Branch .6 mile upstream from Fontana Lake. It provides intermittent access to the stream to 2 miles. The trail reaches Poplar Flats at 2.8 miles and leaves the stream at that point.

Bee Gum Branch

SIZE: small
FISHING PRESSURE: light
FISHING QUALITY: fairly good
USGS QUADS: Noland Creek, NC

Bee Gum Branch is a decent little trout stream. There are a fair number of cascades and pools holding rainbow trout. The stream is heavily overgrown with laurel and rhododendron making fishing difficult.

Access to Bee Gum Branch

Bee Gum Branch flows into the mainstream 2.8 miles upstream from Fontana Lake. Fair access to the stream is provided by the Bee Gum Branch Trail. For the first 2.3 miles the stream is often several hundred yards from the the trail. At 2.8 miles the trail leaves the stream to ascend Forney Ridge.

Jonas Creek

SIZE: small
FISHING PRESSURE: light
FISHING QUALITY: very good
ACCESS: remote
USGS QUADS: Silers Bald, NC-TN

Jonas Creek is a dandy trout stream. Numerous deep holes harbor some fine rainbows. You'll likely have the entire stream to yourself any time you decide to wet a line there. As an added dividend there are several tributaries in this little valley that are very worthwhile to fish. Adventurous anglers can find side streams working alive with trout that seldom see more than a dozen bronzed hooks a year. Two feeder streams of merit are Scarlett Ridge Creek and Little Jonas Creek.

Access to Jonas Creek

The Jonas Creek Trail provides access to the stream. The trailhead is located 4.1 miles upstream from Fontana Lake near the mouth of Jonas Creek. At 1.3 miles the trail forsakes the mainstream and continues upstream alongside Little Jonas Creek, then at 1.7 miles the trail crosses Yanu Branch leaving Little Jonas Creek. The trail then makes a series of switchbacks until 2.7 miles, where it comes within 50 feet of Yanu Branch, before leaving to ascend Welch Ridge.

Huggins Creek

SIZE: small
FISHING PRESSURE: light (closed)
FISHING QUALITY: very good
ACCESS: remote
USGS QUADS: Silers Bald, NC-TN

Huggins Creek is an excellent example of the plight of the Southern Appalachian brook trout. As late as 1975, fish and wildlife surveys showed populations of brook trout in both Huggins Creek and Little Huggins Creek. But present data does not support the presence of brookies in this streamshed.

The four prongs to Huggins Creek begin at an altitude of over 4,800 feet. However, even with such a tributary system it appears the ever encroaching rainbows have perhaps won out.

Access to Huggins Creek

Huggins Creek flows between Suli Ridge and Loggy Ridge. There is an unmaintained trail that begins near the mouth of the stream and follows alongside to the headwaters.

Hazel Creek System

Hazel Creek

SIZE: large

FISHING PRESSURE: lower portion is moderately heavy, upper portion above 2,500 feet is relatively light

FISHING QUALITY: excellent

ACCESS: most easily reached by crossing Fontana Lake

USGS QUADS: Tuskeegee, NC; Thunderhead, NC-TN; Silers Bald, NC-TN

Hazel Creek has been termed "the Crown Jewel" of trout fishing in the Great Smoky Mountains National Park and touted by most major outdoor publications in past years. Hazel Creek has all the needed qualifications to claim being the finest freestone stream in the Southern Appalachian Mountains. One of the secrets of this stream's excellent fishing is the abundant insect life. Caddis flies dominate, although you will find that prolific hatches of *Stenonema* mayflies get the attention of the trout during the summer. The lower portion, dominated by rainbow and brown trout, is highly productive for large terrestrial imitations such as the grasshopper and jassid. Here, the stream rushes past old homesteads and fragrant orchards, forming many long, slow pools, perfect for floating a cinnamon ant pattern. I feel nothing will put the adrenaline in your system faster than a lightning-fast strike from a trout coaxed from one of these beautiful pools.

Brookies can be found in the mainstream beyond an elevation of 3,040 feet, one of the lowest elevations for brookies in a major streamshed in the Smokies. Hazel Creek has one of the loftiest tributary systems in the Park. These headwater streams provide some of the finest brook trout habitat in the Smokies.

Hazel Creek is located in the Southeast section of the Smokies. It is bounded by Welch Ridge and Jenkins Ridge. Its headwaters are located beneath the slopes of Stateline Ridge and from there the stream flows into Fontana Lake. Primary tributaries of Hazel Creek are Sugar Fork, Bone Valley Creek, Walker Creek, and Proctor Creek.

The Hazel Creek watershed was one of the most heavily devastated in the Smokies. The Ritter Logging Company removed virtually every stand of virgin timber from the valley, in an operation that took nearly 20 years. The loggers laid rail lines almost 13 miles up Hazel Creek to enable them to haul the fallen giants to the sawmills. Proctor was a booming sawmill town of over 1,000 people and the center of the valley's life.

Upon receiving stewardship of the Smokies, the National Park Service found many residents reluctant to abandon their mountain homesteads. Even today you may encounter groups of mountain folk on the trail carrying floral arrangements to be placed on graves of loved ones buried in the Park, an annual event for the people who still feel a part of these mountains of their birth.

The forest has regrown nicely under the protection of the National Park Service. The area has an abundance of plant life and, not too surprisingly, many varieties of domestic plant life. Hazel Creek can boast of one of the Park's few beaver colonies. There are no beaver dams on the stream, but the busy beaver have downed a large number of trees alongside the stream, which provide badly needed cover for trout.

Access to Hazel Creek

All roads leading into Hazel Creek were closed during World War II when Fontana Lake was impounded. The isolation has helped spare the stream and enabled it to maintain high-quality fishing.

Crossing the lake by boat is perhaps the easiest and most popular method of visiting Hazel Creek. For a modest sum the operators of the Fontana Village Resort Marina provide transportation across the lake by arrangement. One really nice feature of going this route is being relieved of worrying about the safety of your boat.

You may encounter a variety of strange-looking vehicles on these trails that appear to be a cross between a wheel barrow and bicycle. These versatile contraptions, known as "Smoky Mountain pushcarts," are constructed of light-weight materials such as tubular aluminum and tires from ten-speed bicycles. Such backcountry rarities as coolers full of perishable foods, lanterns, cots, and big tents are transported up the stream in these rigs by local fishermen unwilling to compromise their fishing trips with the usual backcountry fare of freeze-dried foods and cramped hiking tents.

The Hazel Creek Trail follows the stream. The trailhead is located near the mouth of the stream on Fontana Lake. The Proctor backcountry campsite (N.P.S. #86, capacity 20), located .5 mile upstream from the lake, is a popular base camp. Upstream from this site is the "Horseshoe," noted for its excellent trout fishing.

At 3.3 miles is the Sawdust Pile backcountry campsite (N.P.S. #85, capacity 20), also popular with backcountry fishermen. The poetic "Brown Pool" is nearby. Its famous waters have been the sight of the day's last cast for countless anglers.

At 5 miles the trail reaches the junction of Sugar Fork and the trailhead of the Sugar Fork Trail; located nearby is the Sugar Fork backcountry campsite (N.P.S. #84, capacity 8), well suited as a fishing camp. At 5.6 miles the trail arrives at the mouth of Bone Valley Creek, also the trailhead for the Bone Valley Trail and the site of the Bone Valley backcountry campsite (N.P.S. #83, capacity 20). At 8.6 miles the trail reaches the Calhoun Camp backcountry campsite (N.P.S. #82, capacity 15) and continues to the junction of Hazel Creek and Walker Creek at 9.5 miles. The junction of Proctor Creek and the Proctor Creek backcountry campsite (N.P.S. #81, capacity 15) is at 10.5 miles.

The trail upstream from the Proctor Creek site becomes steeper and more difficult to travel. At 13.5 miles the trail reaches the Hazel Creek Cascades backcountry campsite (N.P.S. #80, capacity 12), located at an elevation of over 4,000 feet, well into the heart of the brook trout fishery. The trail upstream from the cascades is steep, though open and passable.

Sugar Fork

SIZE: small
FISHING PRESSURE: fairly light
FISHING QUALITY: very good
ACCESS: you must travel 5 miles up the Hazel Creek Trail
USGS QUADS: Tuskeegee, NC; Thunderhead, NC-TN

Sugar Fork is the first significant feeder stream encountered up Hazel Creek. It's a nice little stream, often overlooked by anglers, offering excellent rainbow trout fishing, with an abundance of cascades that provide interesting fishing most any day of the season.

Haw Gap Branch and Little Sugar Fork are tributaries of angling merit.

Access to Sugar Fork

The Sugar Fork Trail starts 5 miles upstream from the lake. At .5 mile the Sugar Fork Trail reaches the mouth of Haw Gap Branch and the junction of Haw Gap Trail. The Haw Gap Trail offers access to the branch. At 1.7 miles the trail arrives at the junction of Little Sugar Fork. A short distance upstream from this point the trail leaves the stream.

Bone Valley Creek

SIZE: medium
FISHING PRESSURE: moderately light
FISHING QUALITY: excellent
ACCESS: mouth of the stream is over 5.5 miles upstream from the lake
USGS QUADS: Tuskeegee, NC; Thunderhead, NC-TN

Anyone taking the time to visit the Hazel Creek area should spend at least one day exploring and fishing Bone Valley. Bone Valley came by its name in the late 1880s when an unexpected and severe late-spring blizzard hit the area. Cattle, already brought up from the valley, were caught in the midst of the storm's fury. In their efforts to stay warm, the cattle huddled together, one on top of the other. Their efforts failed and huge stacks of bones were left to bleach in the summer sun. Henceforth, the area was known as Bone Valley.

Bone Valley Creek enters the mainstream 5.6 miles upstream from the lake and offers excellent rainbow and brook trout fishing. It is a good-size stream with a challenging mixture of riffles and pools.

Noteworthy tributaries of Bone Valley Creek include Wooly Branch, a good little trout stream, although it is very overgrown; Defeat Branch, a personal favorite, sporting both rainbow and brook trout; Desolation Branch, a brook trout stream; and Roaring Fork, a popular brookie stream.

Access to Bone Valley Creek

The Bone Valley Trail begins at the mouth of the stream, 5.6 miles upstream from the Fontana Lake. The trail follows alongside the stream and reaches the Hall Cabin at 1.7 miles at the end of the maintained portion of the trail, where an unmaintained path continues upstream. At the mouth of Desolation Branch the trail then begins following alongside the small tributary.

Walker Creek

SIZE: small
FISHING PRESSURE: light
FISHING QUALITY: excellent
ACCESS: mouth of the stream is 9.5 miles upstream from Fontana Lake
USGS QUADS: Thunderhead, NC-TN

Walker Creek is a small, often-overlooked trout stream of very good fishing quality. The trout here are of average size but not nearly as leader shy as the fish in the mainstream. There are rainbow trout in the lower section of the stream, but above the falls the stream is all speckled trout.

Access to Walker Creek

The stream is only accessible by an unmaintained path that begins at the mouth of the stream and follows alongside to its headwaters.

Proctor Creek

SIZE: small
FISHING PRESSURE: light
FISHING QUALITY: excellent
ACCESS: mouth of the stream is 10.5 miles upstream from Fontana Lake
USGS QUADS: Thunderhead, NC-TN

Proctor Creek offers anglers a chance to fish in a stream abounding with lively trout amidst an exceptionally beautiful forest setting. This is a popular brook trout stream and barbless hooks are definitely in order for all sportsmen.

Proctor Creek flows into the mainstream 10.5 miles upstream from the lake. This stream has a well-developed tributary system. Long Cove Creek and James Camp Branch are favorites among fishermen.

Access to Proctor Creek

There is an excellent unmaintained path that follows alongside the stream to its headwaters.

Eagle Creek System

Eagle Creek

SIZE: medium

FISHING PRESSURE: moderately light

FISHING QUALITY: very good, particularly upstream from Pinnacle Creek

ACCESS: mouth of the stream is most easily reached by crossing Fontana Lake

USGS QUADS: Fontana Dam, NC; Thunderhead, NC-TN; Cades Cove, NC-TN

Eagle Creek is nestled in a secluded valley in the southwest corner of the Great Smoky Mountains National Park. Its remote location has spared the stream's trout the daily ritual of scanning every morsel for a hidden hook. It receives only a moderate amount of angling pressure, and there are few signs of overuse anywhere in this area. The backcountry campsites are clean and untrampled.

Brook trout still have a few good strongholds in the Eagle Creek watershed, notably Gunna Creek and Asgini Branch. This watershed was not as heavily logged as the nearby Hazel Creek Valley, thus the flow was not defiled by such lethal logging by-products as silt-choked pools and tannic acid (from the decomposing tree bark and slash). Although it is only a matter of conjecture, many knowledgable anglers feel the strong presence of the rainbow trout in the stream is partially responsible for the deterioration of the brook trout fishery.

In recent years a few brown trout have immigrated into the mainstream from Fontana Lake. Their presence is insignificant compared to the abundant rainbow trout that have dominion of the mainstream. Rainbow trout fishing is very good here.

Eagle Creek is bounded by Jenkins Ridge, Stateline Ridge, and Twenty Mile Ridge. It flows into Fontana Lake a short distance from the dam. Eagle Creek's tributaries of interest to fishermen are Lost Creek, Pinnacle Creek, Ekaneetlee Creek, Tub Mill Creek, and Gunnas Creek.

Access to Eagle Creek

Eagle Creek is a roadless watershed, permanently sealed off during World War II by Fontana Lake's impoundment of the Little Tennessee River. Crossing the lake by boat is the most popular means of visiting Eagle. Light boats equipped with small outboard motors or canoes can be rented from the operators of the Fontana Village Resort Marina. Additionally, the operators of the marina will be happy to make arrangements with fishermen to take them to the mouth of the stream and later pick them up. I have made use of this handy service on a number of occasions and highly recommend it.

Anglers wishing to visit Eagle Creek but preferring to keep both feet on solid ground will discover that the Lost Cove Trail offers the easiest access to Eagle Creek from an auto access point. This route makes it necessary to begin on the Appalachian Trail crossing of Fontana Dam. Traveling north along the Appalachian Trail 3.7 miles to Sassafras Gap, the trail reaches the junction of the Lost Cove Trail. The Lost Cove Trail descends down the ridge to the right and at 3 miles reaches the Lost Cove Creek backcountry campsite (N.P.S. #90, capacity 12), a lakeside camp near the mouth of Eagle Creek.

Upstream access is provided by the Eagle Creek Trail, which begins at the mouth of the stream and follows alongside the creek. The trail rounds Horseshoe Bend at .5 mile and reaches the mouth of Pinnacle Creek at 1 mile, also the site of the trailhead for the Pinnacle Creek Trail. The Eagle Creek Trail continues upstream alongside the mainstream to the confluence of Ekaneetlee Creek at 2 miles, where the Lower Ekaneetlee backcountry campsite (N.P.S. #89, capacity 8), a superb fishing camp, is located. Continuing upstream, the Eagle Creek Trail reaches the Eagle Creek Islands backcountry campsite (N.P.S. #99, capacity 10) at 3.5 miles, then continues its upstream climb and at 5 miles reaches the confluence of Tub Mill Creek and Gunna Creek. This is the beginning point of Eagle Creek proper. The Big Walnut backcountry campsite (N.P.S. #97, capacity 10), the last camping spot along the trail, is located here. The Eagle Creek Trail continues upstream alongside Gunna Creek (see Gunna Creek).

Pinnacle Creek

SIZE: small
FISHING PRESSURE: light
FISHING QUALITY: fair
ACCESS: remote
USGS QUADS: Fontana Dam, NC; Thunderhead, NC-TN

Pinnacle Creek is probably the most overlooked feeder stream in the Eagle Creek system. It holds a few good rainbow trout and there is a nice campsite upstream that makes for a fine secluded fishing base.

Access to Pinnacle Creek

The Pinnacle Creek Trail provides good access to the stream. It begins at the mouth of Pinnacle Creek and follows alongside the stream. At 1.5 miles the trail arrives at the Pinnacle backcountry campsite (N.P.S. #88, capacity 8). The trail continues on alongside the stream to 2.8 miles where it leaves the stream and ascends to Pickens Gap.

Ekaneetlee Creek

SIZE: small
FISHING PRESSURE: light
FISHING QUALITY: excellent
ACCESS: remote
USGS QUADS: Fontana Dam, NC; Cades Cove, NC-TN

Ekaneetlee Creek is a fine little trout stream that flows alongside an ancient Indian pathway. There is a good population of speckle trout above the 2,900-foot mark, with rainbows filling the gap between the mainstream and that point.

Big Tommy Branch and Adams Hollow Branch, tributaries of Ekaneetlee Creek, are a sure bet for a day of good fishing.

Access to Ekaneetlee Creek

The Ekaneetlee Manway provides very good access to the stream. Ekaneetlee Creek flows into Eagle Creek 2 miles upstream from Fontana Lake. The trail begins at the mouth of the stream and follows alongside to its headwaters, before ascending to Ekaneetlee Gap. Note: This is an unmaintained trail that is usually kept open by fishermen; however, inexperienced backcountry travelers should exercise caution if they decide to visit here.

Tub Mill Creek

SIZE: small
FISHING PRESSURE: light
FISHING QUALITY: very good
ACCESS: remote
USGS QUADS: Cades Cove, NC-TN

Tub Mill Creek flows together with Gunna Creek to form Eagle Creek. It has a well-developed tributary network that sports both rainbow and brook trout.

Asgini Branch and Lawson Gant Lot Branch, tributaries of Tub Mill Creek, offer good fishing.

Access to Tub Mill Creek

Tub Mill Creek flows into the mainstream 5 miles upstream from Fontana Lake. The stream is reached at this point from the Eagle Creek Trail. There are no maintained trails that lend access upstream from the mouth of the stream.

Gunna Creek

SIZE: small
FISHING PRESSURE: light
FISHING QUALITY: excellent
ACCESS: remote
USGS QUADS: Cades Cove, NC-TN; Thunderhead, NC-TN

Gunna Creek is the upstream extension of the mainstream of Eagle Creek. It holds a mixed population of rainbow and brook trout. Its extreme headwaters were closed to all fishing in 1975 to protect the brook trout that prosper there. Massive hemlocks grow alongside the stream, many covered with cool green growths of thick moss that help make this a delightful place to fish.

Paw Paw Creek and Spence Cabin Branch, tributaries of Gunna Creek, hold populations of colorful speckle trout.

Access to Gunna Creek

The Eagle Creek Trail follows alongside Gunna Creek upstream from its confluence with Tub Mill Creek. The trail passes by the mouth of Paw Paw Creek at 6 miles (upstream from Fontana Lake), then follows alongside this lovely mountain brook 8 miles before leaving, to later terminate upon the ridge at the Appalachian Trail.

Twenty Mile Creek

SIZE: medium
FISHING PRESSURE: moderately light
FISHING QUALITY: good, all season
ACCESS: access to the mouth of the stream is possible at the Park boundary from US 129
USGS QUADS: Tapoco, NC; Fontana, NC

Twenty Mile Creek is one of the least-known streams in the Park. Local anglers have long considered this their secret preserve. The stream is located in the extreme southern portion of the Smokies, isolated from almost all commercial development. Visiting anglers should take the time to discover this gem. Twenty Mile Creek is a productive stream, sporting a scrappy population of rainbow trout in its fast flow. The stream has a nice distribution of deep pools, pocket water, and shallow runs. It's sometimes a challenge to fish, but a well-placed cast will bring rewards.

Twenty Mile Creek is a rainbow trout fishery, although a rare brown trout, up from Cheoah lake, will occasionally be taken in the downstream section. Brook trout are as rare here as chicken teeth.

Twenty Mile Creek is bounded by Wolfe Ridge, Greer Knob, and Twenty Mile Ridge and flows into Cheoah Lake. It is medium size, with a small tributary system. Moore Spring Branch and Dalton Branch offer the best feeder stream fishing in this watershed.

Access to Twenty Mile Creek

The Twenty Mile Creek Ranger Station is located 2.8 miles east of the US 129/NC 28 junction. Drive past the ranger station to the parking area, where the Twenty Mile Creek Trail begins. At .6 mile the trail reaches the mouth of Moore Spring Branch and the junction of the Wolfe Ridge Trail.

The Wolfe Ridge Trail follows Moore Spring Branch, and at 4 miles it arrives at the Wolfe Ridge backcountry campsite (N.P.S. #95, capacity 8). The mouth of Dalton Branch is near this campsite.

The Twenty Mile Creek Trail continues along Twenty Mile Creek and at 1.8 miles arrives at the Twenty Mile backcountry campsite (N.P.S. #93, capacity 14). At 4.5 miles the trail leaves the stream for the last time to ascend Shuckstack Fire Tower.

Abrams Creek System

Abrams Creek

SIZE: at the mouth the stream is large; Cades Cove area is medium
FISHING PRESSURE: moderate to very heavy
FISHING QUALITY: excellent
ACCESS: very accessible by foot
USGS QUADS: Cades Cove, NC-TN; Thunderhead, NC-TN; Calderwood, NC-TN; Blockhouse, TN
REGULATIONS: general; however, Abrams Creek from Mill Creek junction downstream to embayment waters is designated Experimental Fish Management Water and may be fished according to general regulations, except size limit is 7 inches or longer.

Of all the streams in the Great Smoky Mountains National Park, this is my favorite. I have spent many memorable hours on this fine stream and look forward to many more. Abrams Creek is not only the finest rainbow trout stream in the Park but also the most interesting and unique. The spring caddis fly hatches here are equal to any found in the Southern Appalachian Mountains. Abrams Creek can also boast of having one of the Smokies' most spectacular hatches of Quadwing-yellow mayflies. It is not only the fly fishermen who find this stream an inviting haven. The stream is literally working alive with forage fish whose food value to the trout affords the spinner fishermen excellent oportunities.

Abrams Creek is one of many streams in the Park still known by its Indian name. Old Abram was the chief of the Cherokee village of Chilhowee, which was located at the mouth of Abrams Creek on the Little Tennessee River. He met an untimely and gruesome death at the hands of a vengeful 17-year-old lad named John Kirk. Old Abram and four other Cherokee chiefs from the neighboring Citico area were being held prisoners, being thought responsible for the deaths of Kirk's mother and ten brothers and sisters. Kirk entered the lodge where the five chiefs were being held and killed all five with blows from an axe. It was later proved that Creek Indians were responsible for the Kirk family massacre. John Sevier ordered Kirk to be hanged for the murder of the innocent Cherokee leaders, but the flamboyant militiaman refused to allow the execution to be carried out and, subsequently, Kirk was released. John Sevier went on to become the governor of Tennessee, and my great, great, great, great grandfather, John Kirk, resettled much farther north in Nolichucky Valley.

Abrams Creek's headwaters begin on the slopes beneath the grassy balds of Spense Field and Russell Field. The stream from that point flows into Chilhowee Reservoir. The Abrams Creek watershed is located in the southwest section of the Smokies. Its principal tributaries are Panther, Rabbit, and Mill Creeks. Abrams Creek is basically a rainbow/brown trout fishery. Brook trout have almost vanished from this watershed.

The mouth of Abrams Creek is actually part of the Chilhowee Reservoir impoundment. The first couple of miles upstream from the lake offers only mediocre trout fishing. This section of stream is often difficult to travel due to the impoundment and the dense flora around the stream.

It is a common sight in the winter season to view boats full of warmly clad anglers anchored at the mouth of Abrams Creek in Chilhowee Reservoir. These knowledgable fishermen brave the sometimes severe winter weather for a chance at the angling bounty of the rainbow trout spawning run. Winter rains spark the instinctive mating drive of these trout, commonly weighing three to eight pounds, which spend the majority of their lives in the cool depths of the TVA impoundment, waxing fat on forage fish. Before swimming upstream, these hefty milt- and roe-ladden trout often spend a day or two at the mouth of the stream, waiting for precisely the right moment before embarking on their quest. It is during this quasi-immobile period at the mouth of the stream that fishermen often score limits of trout of a much greater size than is generally possible during other times of the year. Great Smoky Mountains National Park regulations prohibit fishing from the banks during the winter months, but Chilhowee Reservoir is open to fishing the year round. Anchoring a boat at the mouth of the stream is both legal and profitable.

Abrams Creek at the Abrams Creek Campground offers excellent trout fishing. The stream has many long green pools, commonly stretching over 300 feet. Here a large number of downed trees litter the stream bank, providing shelter for many wise old mossy-back trout. This section of stream is a favorite haunt of several of the fine local East Tennessee trout fishermen. It is seldom crowded, making this a good bet for a day of solitary fishing.

Upstream from the campground lies an area known as Little Bottoms.

The author fishing
Abrams Creek. Photo
by Joann Kirk.

This is a somewhat remote section of the stream that offers superior trout fishing for those willing to make the two-mile walk. At Abrams Falls the stream plunges 25 feet into a deep emerald pool. The Falls pool harbors many of the stream's largest trout, and the pool's size allows fly fishermen plenty of backcasting room. Unfortunately for anglers, swimmers and sightseers also find Abrams Falls much to their liking. Early morning and late evening are usually the only times anglers can find relative peace on this lovely pool.

Abrams Creek upstream from the Falls to Cades Cove is Smoky Mountains trout fishing at its finest. The stream forms a small loop above the Falls that is seven-tenths of a mile long and requires nearly half a day to properly fish. Immediately upstream, a second loop known as the "Horseshoe" rounds Arbustus Ridge. The Horseshoe is one mile in length and it is advisable to allow a whole day to fish this sometimes tricky stretch of creek. Both the Falls loop and the Horseshoe offer superb trout fishing. The stream is subject to heavy fishing pressure from both sportsmen and poachers. Despite this, rainbow trout in the three- to four-pound class abound. During May, when several species of caddis fly larvae enter the pupae stage and begin darting about beneath the surface, this section of creek literally comes alive with feeding action.

During the spring and winter months the cove section provides good rainbow trout and excellent, but difficult, brown trout opportunities. This area is very overgrown and thoroughly entangled with submerged root structure.

Abrams Creek is better known as Anthony Creek upstream from the Cades Cove Historic Area. Anthony Creek abounds with creel-size rainbow trout. The dense laurel overgrowths surrounding the stream make taking one of these bejeweled little fish a soul-satisfying feat any angler can appreciate. Anthony Creek forks five-tenths of a mile upstream from Cades Cove. The Left Prong originates on the northern slopes of Ledbetter Ridge, and the Right Prong flows off of the slopes of Spense Field. Both prongs of Anthony Creek offer delightful trout fishing amidst a primeval hemlock forest setting.

One of the most unique aspects of Abrams Creek is the metamorphosis the stream undergoes while traversing the Cades Cove Historic Area. Cades Cove sits atop a huge limestone bed. As the creek enters the cove, over 60 percent of the stream filters underground and makes a subsurface passage through the limestone before rejoining the stream near the Abrams Falls parking area. This subsurface trek dramatically increases the stream's generally acidic composition of a pH of 6 to 6.7 to a mild pH of 7.1 to 8.3. The remaining surface-flowing portion of Abrams Creek weaves its way through the Cove's pasture fields where approximately 500 head of cattle are grazed. Here the stream is the recipient of the nutrients from the cattle's waste which rain washes into the stream. These added twists to the stream's composition bring both blessings and problems.

The fecal bacteria from the cattle manure makes the water downstream from the Cove unfit for human use. The near constant presence of the cattle alongside the stream accelerates an already touchy siltation problem. Many gravel spawning beds have been rendered useless by siltation. The silt settles on virtually every rock in the stream making them as hazardous as ice on a winter's day. Wading Abrams Creek is a dangerous adventure even for the most experienced daredevil trout fisherman.

The benefits from the twofold change Abrams Creek is forced to cope with seem to outweigh the problems, at least from the angler's point of view. The added nutrients and the richness gained from the limestone create an ideal habitat for many aquatic invertebrates, particularly the *Trichoptera* (caddis flies). This radical concentration of macroinvertebrates supports a staggering number of rough, forage, and gamefish, especially in the first four miles of flow. Of all the streams in the Smoky Mountains National Park, only Hazel Creek can rival this stream as an angler's paradise.

Access to Abrams Creek

Road access: The Abrams Creek watershed is accessible by automobile from several points. The stream is easily reached from TN 72 where it flows into Chilhowee Reservoir. Access is also available from Abrams Creek Campground which is located 7 miles north of US 129 on the Happy Valley Road.

At Cades Cove there are two primary points of access to the stream. The Abrams Falls parking area allows access to the stream as it leaves the Cove. Access to Anthony Creek can be made from the Cades Cove picnic area.

Trail access: At the Park boundary, near the mouth of Abrams Creek, there is an old unmaintained trail that roughly follows the ascent of the stream. This is the only path to the downstream area. This seldom-traveled trail is often difficult to locate and is not recommended to inexperienced hikers. At some points the trail is seven hundred feet from the stream. At the confluence of Bell Branch, 4 miles upstream from TN 72, the path receives much greater foot travel. The trail from that point weaves alongside Abrams Creek for 2.8 miles to the Rabbit Creek Trail junction.

The Rabbit Creek Trail from the junction point becomes the stream's access trail for anglers. It follows the stream to the Abrams Creek Campground. This facility offers primitive campsite accommodations and is easily reached by auto.

Upstream from the campground, the stream is reached by hiking north on the Cooper Road Trail. The trail leaves the stream .6 mile upstream from the campground. At 1 mile the Cooper Road Trail intersects the Little Bottoms Manway. Located at the trail junction is a spacious backcountry campsite known as Little Bottoms (N.P.S. #17, capacity 10). The Little Bottoms Manway follows the stream up to Abrams Falls Trail. The Falls Trail follows the upstream progress of the stream 2.5 miles to the Falls parking area. There is no trail access to Abrams Creek as it passes through the Cades Cove Historic area.

Anthony Creek, as Abrams Creek is known prior to entering the cove, is accessible from the Anthony Creek Trail. This trail begins at the Cades Cove picnic area. The trail runs adjacent to the stream until the stream forks at 1.5 miles. The Anthony Creek Trail follows the Right Prong of Anthony Creek 2.8 miles before leaving the stream to climb the southern slopes of Cold Water Knob. Located 2.5 miles upstream on the Anthony Creek Trail is the Anthony Creek backcountry campsite (N.P.S. #9, capacity 6).

The Russell Field Trail follows the Left Prong of Anthony Creek upstream 1 mile, then veers right, leaving the stream to ascend Ledbetter Ridge.

Panther Creek

SIZE: medium to small

FISHING PRESSURE: light to moderate

FISHING QUALITY: excellent

ACCESS: via auto from Parsons Branch Road

USGS QUADS: Calderwood, NC-TN

REGULATIONS: this stream is part of Experimental Fish Management Water, may be fished according to general regulations, except size limit is 7 inches or longer

Panther Creek is the first significant tributary encountered upstream from the mouth of Abrams Creek. This is an excellent trout stream, holding a large population of rainbow trout. Although only a fair-size stream, Panther Creek offers a wide variety of stream conditions that can tax even a hardened Appalachian trouter. The downstream portion of the creek receives only a moderate amount of fishing pressure, while upstream near the headwaters, angling pressure is more intense.

Panther Creek begins its seaward journey beneath the southern slopes of High Point. Bear Den Branch, a tributary of Panther Creek, is worthy of mention to trout fishermen. It flows off the slopes of Pole Cat Ridge and literally swarms with fat little rainbow trout that seldom see a feathered hook dangling from a willowy flyrod.

Access to Panther Creek

Panther Creek is accessible by auto from the Parsons Branch Road. This road begins in Cades Cove, off the Loop Road, and crosses Panther Creek at 3.5 miles, at an elevation of 2,540 feet. From this point, anglers are free to fish either upstream or downstream.

The mouth of Panther Creek is reached via an old unmaintained trail, which is a spur trail from the path that connects the Abrams Creek Campground with TN 72. Panther Creek Manway leaves the Abrams Creek Trail at the first stream crossing, and for a short distance follows the downstream progress of Abrams Creek. Hikers must then negotiate a hazardous crossing of Abrams Creek at the mouth of Panther Creek. It is often advisable to make this crossing in a rubber raft or canoe. On the other side of the stream the trail then closely follows the stream 4 miles before leaving the stream to ascend the southern slopes of Bunker Hill. Bear Den Branch flows into the main stream four-tenths of a mile upstream from the trail's last contact with the stream. There is no additional access to the stream until the Parsons Branch Road makes contact with the stream at 2,540 feet.

The Hannah Mountain Trail briefly follows along two small tributaries of Panther Creek; however, neither of these small brooks are of angling merit. There are no backcountry campsites in the Panther Creek system.

Rabbit Creek

SIZE: fairly small
FISHING PRESSURE: light
FISHING QUALITY: good
ACCESS: via Parsons Branch Road
USGS QUADS: Calderwood, NC-TN
REGULATIONS: this stream is part of Experimental Fish Management Water, may be fished according to general regulations, except size limit is 7 inches or longer

Rabbit Creek is one of those nifty little streams trout fishermen become notoriously sullen about when other anglers query them for its secrets. I have never encountered another angler or even evidence of their presence along this rivulet. Rabbit Creek enters Abrams Creek 3.5 miles upstream from the Abrams Creek Campground. Rabbit Creek's icy waters flow from springs located on the sides of Hannah Mountain. Rainbow trout are the dominant species to be found in this stream. There are numerous small tributaries, but none begin at over 2,800 feet. Nearly all of these tiny brooks are inhabited with trout.

Access to Rabbit Creek

Rabbit Creek is accessible from the Parsons Branch Road. This road begins in Cades Cove and runs alongside the stream for over 1 mile. The stream is reached by foot travel from the Rabbit Creek Trail. This trail begins at the Abrams Falls parking area in Cades Cove. The trail reaches the stream at 4.7 miles. At this stream crossing is the popular Rabbit Creek backcountry campsite (N.P.S. #15, capacity 8). This is the only contact with the stream for this trail.

Mill Creek

SIZE: small
FISHING PRESSURE: moderate
FISHING QUALITY: fair
ACCESS: via auto from Cades Cove Loop Road
USGS QUADS: Cades Cove, TN
REGULATIONS: general

Mill Creek flows into Abrams Creek at the Falls parking area. It is most interesting to stand at the junction of these nearly equal-in-size streams and observe the intermingling of their dramatically different waters. Abrams Creek prior to joining Mill Creek is a milky, limestone-rich stream. Its bottom is sandy bedrock. Mill Creek, in sharp contrast, is a crystal-clear, acidic, boulder-strewn rivulet typical of most streams in the Smokies. At the confluence, you can easily observe a marked difference in the streams. To the right, the tinted water of Abrams Creek flows on, holding stubbornly to its former character. To the left, Mill Creek's rusty bottom and clear water fight the inevitable clouding it must undergo. Only after flowing several hundred feet downstream do the two water types intermingle to make each's identity indistinguishable.

Mill Creek is a challenging stream of fair fishing quality. Many of the larger fish instinctively move downstream to Abrams Creek where food is more abundant. Mill Creek is an easy stream to get around on and as an added bonus receives only moderate angling pressure. In early spring, a short jaunt up this creek with a good stone-fly nymph imitation will make you a firm disciple of small-stream trouting. I highly recommend Mill Creek and its tributaries to those wishing a short, easy fishing trip in the Great Smoky Mountains National Park.

Mill Creek's tributaries flow off McCampbell and Forge knobs. Mill Creek forks behind the Becky Cable House in Cades Cove. The right prong is known as Forge Creek, and the left prong is Mill Creek. Forge Creek is also worthy of angling merit. This rocky little branch offers fine fishing to those fishermen deft enough to drop a small fly beneath its many foaming cascades. Ekaneetlee Branch, a tributary to Forge Creek, holds a population of rainbow trout. This is a very small creek, but one with a good sprinkling of cascade pools of surprising depth. It's a good stream to depend on for a meal of fresh trout if you plan a backcountry trip in that area.

Access to Mill Creek

Mill Creek is accessible by automobile from the Abrams Falls parking area, the Becky Cable House, and the Forge Creek Road, all of which are off the Cades Cove Loop Road. The Forge Creek Road follows the upstream ascent of Forge Creek to 1,929 feet before leaving the stream for the last.

An old unmaintained road follows Mill Creek 1 mile, after which there is no other trail access. The old road begins off the Forge Creeks Road near the last crossing of Mill Creek.

An old unmaintained road follows Mill Creek 1 mile, after which there is no other trail access. The old road begins off the Forge Creek Road near the last crossing of Mill Creek.

Forge Creek is accessible from the Gregory Ridge Trail which begins at the stream's last contact with the Forge Creek Road. This trail follows alongside the stream 2 miles to 2,600 feet. The Ekaneetlee Manway offers access to Ekaneetlee Branch. This trail begins off the Gregory Ridge Trail behind the Big Poplar, which is about 2 miles from the trailhead. There is a backcountry campsite (N.P.S. #12, capacity 8), known as Ekaneetlee, five-tenths of a mile upstream on the trail. Note: The Ekaneetlee Manway is an unmaintained trail that should only be used by experienced hikers and trout fishermen.

Minor Stream Systems
of the Smokies

Besides the major watersheds, anglers may also fish a number of small streamsheds that begin within, but do not flow into, a larger system, prior to departure from the Park. They vary in size from hard-to-find Tabcat Creek, which flows from the extreme southern end of the Park, to Parson Branch, a respectable-size creek with excellent auto access. Many of these little streams are seldom fished by anyone other than local anglers, although most offer fair to very good angling. These streams are broken down into two sections—Tennessee and North Carolina. Most should be considered early-season picks; it is not uncommon for these streams to shrink to little more than a trickle during the dry periods of summer.

TENNESSEE

Cosby Creek

SIZE: small
FISHING PRESSURE: moderate
FISHING QUALITY: fair
ACCESS: easily reached where it flows out of the Park by TN 32
USGS QUADS: Luftee Knob, NC; Hartsford, TN

Few places in the Southern Appalachians compare with the colorful community of Cosby. In years past this hilly hamlet laid a valid claim on the distinction of being the "Moonshine Capital of the World." Today the storied cornmash distillery businessmen are difficult to locate, having forsaken runnin' 'shine for other forms of livelihood.

Cosby Creek is a small stream draining a surprisingly large basin bounded by the lofty peaks Mt. Cammerer and Mt. Inadu. The creek's lower reaches are populated by rainbow trout, while brookies still hold sway over the headwaters. This is one of the more scenic streams in the Park, cascading over moss-encrusted boulders and passing under a canopy of hemlocks. Fishing quality is fair to poor where the creek flows past the Cosby Campground, a developed area offering 230 campsites. The middle and headwater reaches, including the tributaries of Crying Creek, Tom's Creek, Inadu Creek, and Rock Creek, offer slightly better opportunity.

Access to Cosby Creek

Cosby Creek flows under TN 32, 20 miles east of Gatlinburg, adjacent to the entrance to the Park at the Cosby Campground Road. Upstream access from the Park boundary to the campground is available via Cosby Campground Road, which travels alongside the creek.

The Cosby Creek Trail follows the stream after it leaves the road (the trailhead is located in the southeast corner of the Cosby Campground) for 1 mile before leaving the creek for the last time.

Indian Camp Creek

SIZE: small
FISHING PRESSURE: closed in 1975
FISHING QUALITY: very good
ACCESS: reached from the Laurel Springs Road, off TN 73, 15.3 miles east of Gatlinburg
USGS QUADS: Jones Cove, TN; Mt. Guyot, TN

Indian Camp Creek, one of the most popular brookie streams in the Park prior to the 1975 Brook Trout Moratorium, flows past nearby Albright Grove, where a magnificent virgin stand of poplars tower. Although Indian Camp Creek will probably remain closed to all fishing for some time, anglers are urged to make the 3-mile hike back to this wonderland to view the splendor of an uncut Southern forest.

Access to Indian Camp Creek

The Indian Camp Creek Trail lends access to a portion of Indian Camp Creek. The trailhead is located off Laurel Springs Road, a gravel road that junctions with TN 73, 15.3 miles east of Gatlinburg. The trail crosses Cole Creek and Maddron Creek, tributaries of Indian Camp Creek, before reaching the mainstream at 2.7 miles. Driving from Gatlinburg, as you pass the 15-mile mark you will observe the Rainbow Ranch, a pay-to-fish pond on the right. Laurel Springs Road enters the highway near this establishment. The trailhead is a few hundred yards beyond.

Dunn Creek

SIZE: small
FISHING PRESSURE: closed in 1975
FISHING QUALITY: good
ACCESS: passes under TN 73, 14.5 miles east of Gatlinburg
USGS QUADS: Jones Cove, TN; Mt. Guyot, TN

Six prongs of this lovely rivulet begin at an altitude of over 4,400 feet along the steep slopes of Pinnacle Lead. Brook trout are still fairly common in the upper reaches of this little branch.

An old-timer from the Cosby community told me that at one time, as many as 15 moonshine stills operated along this branch and its prongs during the late 1940s.

Access to Dunn Creek

There are no maintained trails that cross or follow the stream, although there was at one time an old path alongside it for several miles.

Webb Creek

SIZE: small
FISHING PRESSURE: light
FISHING QUALITY: fair to questionable
ACCESS: passes under TN 73, 13.5 miles east of Gatlinburg
USGS QUADS: Jones Cove, TN; Mt. Guyot, TN-NC; Gatlinburg, TN

Webb Creek differs from the majority of waters described because its flow within the Great Smoky Mountains National Park consists of several small brooks that later merge with the mainstream outside the Park. The mainstream of Webb Creek leaves the Park 13.5 miles east of Gatlinburg, passing under TN 73 as a small brook, having originated between the steep slopes of Snag Mountains and Pinnacle Lead. A number of very small feeder streams flowing out of the Park pass under TN 73 to enter Webb Creek downstream from the Park boundary. These streams include Texas Creek, a very small waterway with two prongs extending over 4,000 feet in elevation; Nosy Creek, one of the largest of the feeder streams, with four prongs that each pass the 4,000-foot mark; Redwine

Creek and Timothy Creek, both very small but lovely brooks; and Soak Ash Creek. Most have rainbow trout averaging less than seven inches in length.

Access to Webb Creek

Webb Creek is reached from the Park boundary upstream, only by moving along the trailless creek. The creek flows under TN 73, 13.5 miles east of Gatlinburg.

Hesse Creek

SIZE: medium
FISHING PRESSURE: light
FISHING QUALITY: fair to good
ACCESS: fairly remote
USGS QUADS: Kinel Springs, TN; Blockhouse, TN

Hesse Creek is the largest of the streams noted in this chapter, draining one of the most unique and least-visited regions of the Smokies. Hesse Creek Valley is often referred to as the Hurricane, probably because of severe blow-downs that have occurred here in the past.

The Hurricane is best known for its caves and unusual flora. Logged in the early part of the nineteenth century by the Little River Logging Company, Hesse Valley has today regrown nicely. One of the more unique items fishermen will note are the lush cane breaks growing along the streams. The cane, actually a species of bamboo, *Arundinaria tecta,* was especially favored by old-time fishermen as excellent material for making fishing poles.

The quality of fishing in this watershed is fair to very good. There are plenty of trout here, although they average under eight inches in length. Noteworthy tributaries of Hesse Creek include Cane Creek and Bread Cane Creek.

Note: National Park Service regulations forbid the removal of any plant (or part thereof) from the Park.

Access to Hesse Creek

There is no easy way of entering the Hurricane. All routes require a moderate amount of foot travel. Hesse Creek, upon leaving the Great Smoky Mountains National Park, flows through a lovely rural area known as Miller Cove. The Miller Cove Road (which junctions with TN 73 near the intersection of the highway and the Foothills Parkway) dead-ends 1 mile from the Park boundary. An old unmaintained path continues upstream alongside Hesse Creek. Cane Creek (which originates in the Park) enters the mainstream at .7 mile from the right (another unmaintained path begins at its mouth and follows the upstream ascent of Cane Creek, later junctioning with the Cooper Road Trail).

The path continues alongside Hesse Creek, entering the Park at 1 mile, and at 1.3 miles arrives at the mouth of Bread Cane Creek. The Bread Cane Creek Trail follows alongside Bread Cane Creek to its headwaters, before terminating at 2.5 miles at the Cooper Road Trail. Further upstream progress along Hesse Creek is limited to trailless travel.

Tabcat Creek

SIZE: small
FISHING PRESSURE: light
FISHING QUALITY: fair
ACCESS: flows into Calderwood Lake 2.5 miles south of the mouth of Abrams Creek on TN 72
USGS QUADS: Calderwood, TN-NC

Tabcat Creek is one of the least-known quality trout streams in the Park. Early spring is the best time to venture up this seldom-trampled stream, as it is quite small, and during the dry periods common to the late summer, it often appears to nearly dry up. Rainbow trout in the six- to nine-inch range are plentiful; fishable tributaries include Bunker Hill Branch and Maynard Creek.

Access to Tabcat Creek

Tabcat Creek flows into Calderwood Lake 2.5 miles south of the mouth of Abrams Creek on TN 72. There is an old unmaintained path that begins at the Park boundary and follows Tabcat Creek to the confluence of Bunker Hill Branch, later reaching Bunker Hill.

Parson Branch

SIZE: medium
FISHING PRESSURE: moderately light
FISHING QUALITY: fair
ACCESS: accessible for a large portion of its flow within the Park by auto via one-way Parson Branch Road, which begins in Cades Cove
USGS QUADS: Calderwood, TN-NC; Tapoco, TN-NC

Parson Branch is the sort of stream a trout fisherman passes on a Sunday drive with the family and swears to return and fish later on, but never does. The stream holds a good population of rainbow trout, most fairly small. Black Gum Branch, a tributary of Parson Branch, also offers fair fishing.

Access to Parson Branch

Parson Branch flows into Calderwood Lake after leaving the Park. The Parson Branch Road, a one-way gravel road originating off the Cades Cove Loop Road, provides excellent roadside access to most of the mainstream, following the stream from its headwaters to the Park boundary.

NORTH CAROLINA

Chambers Creek

SIZE: small
FISHING PRESSURE: moderately light
FISHING QUALITY: good
ACCESS: remote
USGS QUADS: Noland Creek, NC

Chambers Creek offers fairly good trout-fishing opportunities for those wishing to make the trip across Fontana Lake. There is an excellent backcountry campsite (Chambers Creek, N.P.S. #98, capacity 10) that serves fishermen nicely as a base camp. The stream is populated with rainbow trout, with brook trout reputed to be in the extreme headwater reaches. The North Fork and the West Fork merge .7 mile upstream from Fontana Lake to form the Chambers Creek. Both offer good trout fishing.

Access to Chambers Creek

Chambers Creek is located between Forney and Hazel creeks. It is most often visited by crossing Fontana Lake and is easily recognized by the long cove that cushions it from the main body of the lake.

An unmaintained fisherman's trail ascends the creek. Upon reaching the junction of the North and West Forks at .7 mile the trail also forks, with footpaths following both small rivulets for a short distance.

Cooper Creek

SIZE: small
FISHING PRESSURE: light
FISHING QUALITY: good
ACCESS: Cooper Creek Trail offers fair access to the stream
USGS QUADS: Smokemont, NC

Cooper Creek is a noisy little rivulet tucked between two better-known watersheds, the Oconaluftee River and Deep Creek, and offers pretty fair angling for rainbow trout. Cooper Creek is relatively small, but those looking for an out-of-the-way locale in which to wet a line should not mark this little gem off their list.

Access To Cooper Creek

The Cooper Creek Trail offers good access to the most productive reaches of the stream. Its trailhead is located .4 mile upstream from the termination of the Cooper Creek Road, which junctions with US 19, 5.5 miles southwest of Cherokee.

The trail travels along the route of the stream 1.8 miles before leaving the creek. An unmaintained path continues alongside the stream for a distance.

Fontana Lake

Perched almost 2,000 feet above sea level, Fontana Lake is one of the "highest" impoundments in the seven-state Tennessee Valley Authority. This 10,530-surface-acre lake sits wedged between the Great Smoky Mountains National Park and the Nantahala National Forest. During the summer months when the surrounding countryside is dominated by forest green and cloud-dotted pale blue skies, this emerald-green lake appears natural, sometimes giving the impression of being a jewel in a fine piece of jewelry.

Needless to say, Fontana Lake is a superbly scenic man-made lake. Development along this impoundment of the Little Tennessee River, though far from nonexistent, is limited. In 1985 there were six marinas along the lake's shoreline offering the standard array of boat dock services (gas, snacks, boat rentals, launching ramp, and, in some cases, guide service). A list of these boat docks is provided in table 2.

Physically, the lake gives the impression of greater altitude than of slightly less than 2,000 feet above sea level. There are no significant aquatic weeds here and little in the way of fish-holding structure other than rock and gravel. The exception to this is a fish attractor program carried out by TVA and North Carolina. This unique program is in essence a man-made structure, usually in the form of downed trees or brush piles. These sites concentrate fish 9 to 19 times greater than an unmanipulated shoreline.

Fontana Lake is a result of the impoundment of the Little Tennessee River which drains western North Carolina. The Little "T" River is formed by such well-known Carolina rivers as the Tuckasegee, Nantahala, and Oconaluftee rivers. Primary feeder streams entering Fontana Lake along the north shore from the Great Smoky Mountains National Park are Eagle, Hazel, Chambers, Forney, and Noland creeks, while on the south shore, the major feeder streams entering from the Nantahala

Table 2: Fontana Lake Boat Docks

Name & address	River mile	Gas & oil	Food	Lodging	Launch
Fontana Dock Highway 28 P.O. Box 68 Fontana Dam, NC 28733	62.5	*	*	*	*
Crisp Dock Almond, NC 28702	74.5	*	*	*	*
Panther Creek Dock Robinsville, NC 28771	74.5	*	*	*	*
Greasy Creek Dock Bryson City, NC 28713	81.2	*	*	*	*
Alarka Boat Dock 7230 Grassy Branch Road Bryson City, NC 28713	81.5	*	*	*	*
Almond Boat Park 1165 Almond Boat Park Road Bryson City, NC 28713	85.1	*	*	*	*

National Forest are Panther, Alarkaand, and Stecoah creeks.

This is a storage-type impoundment that is drawn down over 50 feet each year. The lake is held at a low level during the autumn and winter to accommodate potentially heavy seasonal rainfall. Lake levels begin rising during the early spring, with full pool (1,709-foot elevation, maximum) usually achieved between May and July. A gradual drawdown usually begins in mid- to late July, although all the above water level data are dependant on annual rainfall as well as power and downstream navigational needs.

Fontana Dam's construction began overnight following the United State's entrance into World War II in late 1941. The TVA was nearly ten years old when the Fontana project began, having already begun a number of projects in the Tennessee River Valley. High-voltage power needs at defense plants in nearby Alcoa, Tennessee, for war plane construction, as well as a then top-secret project taking shape in Oak Ridge, Tennessee (where the first atomic bomb was assembled), proved to be the impetus behind the dam's crash-building program.

Many thousand of acres of bottomland and ridge country were purchased from local residents, many of whom were less than willing to turn over family holdings to the federal government. Much of these tracts became the lake and immediate ground, although 44,204 acres acquired from the mountain folk were later deeded over to the Great Smoky

Mountains National Park. Today this property forms the sometimes controversial north shore, Hazel Creek area. An additional 11,667 acres acquired along the lake's southern shoreline were later transferred to the U.S. Forest Service.

Less than a month after the bombing of Pearl Harbor the first construction crews began arriving at the sleepy mountain hamlet known as Fontana Village. Legislation passed through Congress prior to the hostilities for a dam atop the Little Tennessee River in Graham County, North Carolina, had paved the way for the project's beginning. This legislation was not adequate warning though for what was to ensue over the coming months. Survey crews arrived first, followed by building crews who immediately began putting up housing for the soon-to-arrive 7,000 construction workers and support crews who worked on the dam on an around-the-clock, 24-hours-a-day, seven-days-a-week basis. To accommodate the influx of construction workers, engineers, support personnel and their families, in addition to housing and dormitories, cafeterias, stores, laundries, and even movie houses and schools were built. The construction camp bore the name Fontana Village. Even during the war era when gas rationing and extremely poor mountain roads slowed most travel, well over 1 million Tennessee and North Carolina residents made the trip here to witness this much-heralded building project.

Fontana Dam. TVA photo.

Building Fontana Dam was an engineering accomplishment of astonishing merit. It ranks as the tallest dam east of the Rockies, standing 480 feet high from top to bottom, yet it took only slightly over two years to complete this remote dam. The project's cost was only $71 million, a mere fraction of what such a gigantic undertaking would cost today!

The completed Fontana Dam construction project left TVA with a new, ready-to-operate hydroelectric/flood control facility and a white elephant construction ghost town. Even before the project's completion, federal and state officials had realized Fontana Village's recreational possibilities. The war years were, unfortunately, an inopportune time to kick off a tourism project and for several years only dam maintenance crews resided here.

During the late forties Guest Service Inc., a Washington, D.C.–based non-profit corporation with experience in operating recreational ventures in a number of western national parks, leased the Fontana Village complex from TVA and has operated it as a family vacation resort since that time.

Personally, we have stayed at Fontana Village many times over the years, and have made return trips to that quaint low-development area an annual trip. Two things about Fontana Village make it different from virtually all other Southern Appalachian vacation spots. First, much of the rustic nature found here when Fontana Village was a backwoods construction camp still exists. The worker cabins and cottages have been remodeled and are now guest lodging, but their rough-hewn character still glimmers through. The old cafeteria still serves up homemade fruit pies and biscuits 'n' gravy as it did daily 40 years ago, and the old movie house that once flickered Bogie and John Wayne movies across its silver screen still shows the latest movies. Modern amenities abound, but much of the village's former self is openly visible.

Fontana Village's other unique attribute is its locale and proximity to the finest treasure house of the Southern highlands. One has only to walk a few hundred feet from any point here to enjoy the region's lush flora. The Appalachian Trail passes directly through the village, and other trails and noteworthy backcountry destinations are easily reached from this place.

Coupled with a low-key approach and the area's total lack of competing development, when staying here one gets a strong feeling of having stepped back in time 50 years.

Fishing is without question Fontana Lake's number-one drawing card. Angling is nearly always very good here, and the lake's setting amidst such splendid mountains makes even certain-to-occur fishless days easy to swallow.

Fontana Lake sports a surprisingly diverse gamefish fishery for a mountain lake. Angling for smallmouth bass, walleye, white bass, rainbow and steelhead trout, muskie (and tiger muskie), and bream is on a par with lakes anywhere. Catfish are also plentiful, and fishing for largemouth bass, brown trout, red breast bream and crappie rates fair to good.

Much of Fontana Lake's nationally recognized fishing reputation grew around this lake's smallmouth bass fishery. While everyone has their own opinion of which gamefish is the top battler when stung by a hook (and I might add I'm a dyed-in-the-wool trout fisherman), most angling surveys end with the smallmouth bass at the top of the list . . . and rightfully so! The acrobatics these chunky muscle-bound fish put on each time they are hooked is enough to inspire even the most jaded trout fisherman.

Fontana Lake, with its steep, rocky shoreline and year-round cool water temperatures, is picture-perfect bronzeback habitat. Bronzebacks in the 10- to 14-inch class are the usual fare, but big smalljaws in the three-pound class are always a possibility, and tackle busters in the four- to six- and even seven-pound class inhabit every rocky point.

The best smallmouth bass fishing occurs between mid-April and late June. This time slot encompasses the smallie's early-season awakening. Movement into small feeder creek areas takes place first, followed by the nesting time along the gravel shoreline areas.

Bait fishing with live, three-inch minnows is a productive early-season ploy, while later in the season such crankbaits as Rebel's deep running Crawdad or the Bomber II are lethal when worked adjacent to the shoreline. Throughout this period these bass are relatively shallow (two to ten feet deep) and easily accessible to the average angler.

Hot weather and "long-day sunshine" send the smallmouth bass deep from July through September, with average depths being 10 to 35 feet deep during the daylight hours. During these months the fish can be taken on red, purple, or black plastic worms, as well as brown, black, or purple spider jigs with #101 Uncle Josh pork rinds. Because deep-structure fishing with these bottom chunking baits is difficult and usually frustrating for inexperienced anglers, many Fontana Lake bass fishermen turn to the twilight hours when the brown bass return to the shallows to feed.

Nighttime small and largemouth bass fishing here can be outstanding. A variety of baits ranging from deep-water hardware to medium-depth running crankbaits or even top-water baits are used during the twilight hours. Live bait, particularly spring lizards or night crawlers fished off rocky points, are also good nocturnal bass takers. These varied twilight fishing methods are consistently used by knowledgable local bass anglers throughout the autumn months.

Largemouth bass are readily available throughout Fontana Lake even though this impoundment is seldom touted for its green hawg fishery. Granted, the bigmouth bass are not caught as frequently as the smalljaws, but they are actively sought here by bass tourney anglers seeking to accumulate quick poundage during competition.

Techniques used to take Fontana's bronzebacks are solid ploys for "ole bucket mouth." Holding areas for both are closer on Fontana Lake than on most large/smallmouth bass lakes due to this lake's steep-walled disposition. There are a few mud flats in the headwaters preferred by the warmer-natured largemouth bass during the spring, but generally speaking these fish are lumped into the same general areas, which in turn makes the tactics and baits used for the bronzeback quite effective for its larger-growing cousin.

Fontana Lake has a long-standing reputation as an outstanding walleye fishery. These large-growing perch were native to the Little "T" River drainage prior to this lake's creation and have prospered well here. Late winter finds these river-spawning fish in the swift headwaters of the Little "T," Nantahala, and Tuckasegee rivers. Trampling the riverbanks casting green or yellow quarter-ounce leadhead jigs or live minnows along the rocky bottom is the best way to catch a mess of spawning run marbeleyes.

These fish return downstream into the lake by April, feeding in 2- to

Fontana Lake rates high as a walleye fishing hot spot. Photo by Joann Kirk.

13-feet-deep water near the shoreline. Casting night crawlers, minnows, or green half- to quarter-ounce feather jigs to the bank and "stair casing" the bait down during the early and late hours are the most productive techniques. These techniques are good through late spring when warmer weather sends the walleye progressively deeper. Trolling creek embayments, especially Hazel and Forney, is super-effective.

During the summer months the most serious walleye fishing occurs under the stars in the lake's lower forth. Vertically jigging spoons or dollflies as well as dabbling live minnows under a lantern extended over the water are bonafide tricks for taking these delicious fish. The area immediately adjacent to the dam and Eagle Creek are top walleye spots for lantern fishing. Walleye up to seven pounds are sometimes caught here.

Many anglers visit this lake to explore its little-touted trout fishery. Rainbow trout originally descended Fontana's well-known trout streams Hazel, Noland, and Forney, while subsequent stocking of these fish have resulted in a first-class lake rainbow trout fishery. Recent introduction of steelhead rainbow trout by North Carolina fishery managers has provided a relatively new fishery for these "sea run" 'bows, which hopefully will achieve greater growth than the stream-oriented rainbows common to Fontana's open-water environment. The lake also contains a little-fished-for, generally overlooked brown trout population.

Late winter and early spring finds these cold-natured exotics in the headwaters of the lake's numerous feeder streams. This is spawning time for these trout (except the browns) and swift-moving water is required for mating success. While actual spawning takes place in the upstreams from the lake (see chapters on Hazel, Forney, Eagle, and Noland creeks), good rainbow trout catches always occur in the creek mouths where these fish "stage" in large numbers prior to ascending the current.

Small spinners, a large variety of live and other baits, as well as small silver-hued shallow- and medium-depth running crankbaits are all good at this time. During late winter and spring these fish are not overly aggressive, but persistence and keeping your bait wet will usually undo these fish. Most trout caught from Fontana Lake are commonly taken in excess of five pounds!

Fontana Lake's trout become roamers during the summer and autumn months, frequenting open water and large creek embayments. Hot weather sends trout deep, up to 50 feet down during the dog days. During the summer's daylight (and night) hours deep trolling spoons such as Dardevles' Go Devil are hot. As with the walleye, moonlight fishing under a suspended lantern is productive using spoons and live minnows.

One of the most popular and abundant gamefish found in this highland lake is the white bass. Each spring during April nearly everyone stops fishing for black bass, walleye, and trout to make trips to the

White bass are numerous in Fontana Lake and provide great angling fun during April. Photo by Joann Kirk.

headwaters to cash in on the white bass's river-spawning run. Daily catches in excess of a hundred white bass, or stripe as most locals refer to these true bass, are common.

The North Carolina state record white bass, a compact 4-pound, 15-ounce specimen, was taken from Fontana Lake in 1966. When early-spring water temperatures reach the mid-fifties, these gregarious two- to three-pound fish ascend from the lake to spawn in the Tuckasegee, Little "T," and Nantahala rivers. Small white, yellow, or green leadhead jigs or light, single-blade spinners in white and red are deadly river-run white bass baits, along with live minnows.

River-spawning whites are aggressive fish that station themselves in the shoals and pools. Casting across the current and briskly retrieving your offering is the favorite method. Fly fishermen can have great fun using bright streamers and weight forward, sinking line.

During the rest of the year the lake's white bass roam the open water in great schools ripping up shallow shad school. These fish remain shallow (2 to 15 feet deep) throughout the hot-weather months. Top-water action using small silver crankbaits can be fun when the whites are in the "jumps" feeding on surface shad, and night fishing under lanterns using minnows is also popular.

Muskie were once common throughout the mainstream reaches of this lake's headwaters but nearly disappeared when water quality began to suffer in the early portion of the twentieth century and were virtually KO'd when the valley's system of dams was built. Muskie are large-growing fish, commonly weighing over 20 pounds. They are strong, sharp-toothed predators believed to kill other fish simply for sport. I once spoke with a man on the now-lost Little "T" downstream from Chilhowee Dam, who related he had been crippled by a big muskie in that river during his youth. He had been wading and fishing in short trousers when a toothsome muskie came up behind him and ripped the muscles from the back of one leg! This in itself is a somewhat unusual occurrence (though not rare!), but it does illustrate the muskie's highly aggressive and unpredictable nature.

Muskie were stocked in Fontana Lake several years ago and have become quite popular there. A muskie/northern pike hybrid, the tiger muskie, or mountain tiger as this crossbred is called here, has also been intensively planted in Fontana Lake. The present state record fish for both species was taken from this lake. The muskie record was taken in 1982 by a youth fishing 'doughballs, weighted at 29 pounds, 8 ounces, while the North Carolina record tiger muskie, a fat 21-pound, 10-ounce fish was taken in 1980.

Muskie are legendary for their difficulty in coaxing to the hook. Add to this the fact that these are solitary, highly territorial predators requiring over 100 acres of hunting space. Even prime muskie water is limited in the number of trophy-class fish it can support.

Winter and spring are considered the best times to vie with these fish. The two most popular ploys are trolling creek embayments and around main channel points with large spoons and five- to nine-inch minnow-type crankbaits. Other knowledgable muskie anglers here spend their time point-fishing using large, live creek chubs. Both methods are slow to produce action, sometimes requiring a week of Job-like patience before the first strike is registered, but these are the lake's largest gamefish and well worth the effort if your preference is to go first class.

Fontana Lake is seldom noted as a top-flight catfish lake, but channel and flathead cats abound throughout this impoundment. The state record channel cat, a 40.5-pound whiskered monster, was taken from the lake in 1971. Catfish are a year-round fish even though most angling for these tasty fish takes place during the late summer.

Winter finds these fish deep in the main channel. Although catfish are rarely written about as schooling fish, they do follow migration routes from the lake's tailwaters upstream and then into the major creek embayments to mate during late July.

Trollers and bass fishermen take a great many catfish without even trying, because these fish will readily strike flies and plugs. Serious catfish followers play on the cat's well-developed sense of smell, opting for "stink" baits concocted from chicken liver or cut shad internals. Trotlines or jug fishing in a back cove will sometimes net up to a hundred pounds of catfish in a single night on this productive lake.

Crappie are found throughout Fontana Lake, but these ever-popular panfish are not as abundant here as in many nearby lakes. Relatively good April and May slabside fishing does occur here when the dogwoods are in bloom, and the state and TVA fish attractor brush piles are always the hot spots. Recent TVA maps of Fontana Lake (available at a minimal charge by writing the TVA Map Sales Office, Haney Building, Chattanooga, TN 37401) show the locations of these man-made fish attractors.

Bluegill and redbreast bream are probably the most sought after vacation time fish species at Fontana Lake. Live crickets or red worms dabbled beneath a bobber along most any shoreline will net even a three-year-old enough delicious sunfish to feed a family. During the spring these fish are generally concentrated in extreme back-cove areas under shoreline debris. During the late June/July bream nesting period, shallow backwater areas are sought out. For late-summer "trophy" bluegill action, try tight-lining bait deep (7 to 15 feet deep) along main channel cliffs and rock bluffs.

Camping is popular around Fontana Lake. Backcountry camping is permitted along the north shore in the Great Smoky Mountains National Park on a permit basis. This is "tent only" camping, and only a limited number of people per site are permitted. These include Lost Cove along the Eagle Creek embayment, Proctor along the Hazel Creek embayment, Kirkland Creek at the mouth of Kirkland Creek, Hicks Branch between Kirkland and the mouth of Chambers Creek, Chambers Creek along the Chambers Creek embayment, Lower Forney along the Forney Creek embayment, Goldmine Branch along the Goldmine Branch embayment, and Lower Noland Creek inland along the narrow Noland Creek embayment. These campsites are popular and often full. Also, many are readily accessible by boat only when the lake is at full pool.

The U.S. Forest Service maintains two well-developed campgrounds along Fontana Lake's southern shoreline. Cable Cove Campground, located near the mouth of Rattlesnake Branch and accessible from US 19 approximately two miles east of Fontana Village, offers boat access, sanitary facilities and trailer spaces. Tsali Campground located in the lake's Little Tennessee River arm offers the same services. Both are well maintained and highly recommended.

The Finger Lakes
of the Smokies

Wine connoisseurs fond of New York State white and sparkling wines probably believe the U.S.'s only "finger lakes" are those glacial afterthoughts found in the Empire State. Not so, and if you don't believe this, just look at the Great Smoky Mountains National Park's southern edge.

Found here are three slender, snaking lakes: Cheoah, Calderwood, and Chilhowee, the Finger Lakes of the South. Unlike nearly all other nearby man-made lakes in the Tennessee River drainage, this string of Little Tennessee River impoundments is not part of the gigantic Tennessee Valley Authority system. Each is owned and operated by Tapoco, a subsidiary of the Aluminum Company of America (or Alcoa).

These are old impoundments. Cheoah Dam was completed in 1919; Calderwood was finished and ready to operate in 1930; and Chilhowee was finished in 1959. Being located between the Great Smoky Mountains National Park and Nantahala and Cherokee National Forest (as well as corporate properties) has served to make development along these lakes virtually nonexistent. There are no marinas, no restaurants, no gas stations, and only a very, very few lodging stations near the lakes' collective 27-mile length alongside US 129 and US 19. While this is certainly an inconvenience of sorts for some, the lakes' surrounding raw nature is a solace to most.

All three impoundments have scenic qualities rarely found in man's handy work, and more important to anglers, each holds loads of brightly silvered trout. It would be easy to lump these lakes together, but each differs from the others in a variety of ways.

Sound interesting? You bet it is!

Cheoah Lake

Cheoah was the first impoundment built on the Little Tennessee River, predating the creation of the Tennessee Valley Authority by almost 15 years. The dam's hydroelectric-producing capabilities are quite substantial despite its age, with the bulk of its production power being consumed by Alcoa for the production of aluminum. This old dam is visible where US 129 crosses Calderwood Lake near Tapoco.

Cheoah Lake extends approximately ten miles behind 189-foot-high Cheoah Dam. Despite the dam's impressive height, much of the lake is silt filled, with its winding main channel and the area near the Santeetlah Powerhouse being the lake's deepest zones.

The Finger Lake area along the Little Tennessee River was one of the primary cultural centers of the Overhill Cherokee. These tribes were forcibly removed from the eastern United States during the late 1830s. By the time of the Civil War this area was completely settled, although it was never crowded. The Little Tennessee River's course was a natural route for railways, and logging trains made daily treks out this way by the end of the nineteenth century. Only the rising water from these lakes halted timber operations in a number of otherwise remote watersheds. Today this area is fully forested and displays a wild look seldom found around man-made lakes.

Beginning beneath the concrete walls of Fontana Lake, Cheoah is fed year round with cold, clean water. This fact makes Cheoah Lake one of the coldest, if not *the* coldest, impoundments south of the Mason-Dixon line.

Trout are the lakes' primary gamefish, and this lake is stocked regularly by the state of North Carolina with rainbow, brown, and brook trout. Although food is not as abundant here as in Fontana, Cheoah's trout grow reasonably fast, and this lake environment achieves large sizes. 7- to 9-inch rainbows and browns are common, and larger browns up to 4 to 6 pounds are available in good numbers. The brookies usually do not grow longer than a foot but by Southern stream standards this is large.

Cheoah Lake's major feeder streams are Lewellyn Branch, a small tributary that enters the lake near the US 19 bridge, and Twenty Mile Creek, a major stream that enters four miles upstream from Cheoah Dam. Both drain the high country in the Great Smoky Mountains National Park.

Icy water from Santeetlah Lake several miles away, yet connected to Cheoah Lake via a pipeline, descends 663 feet before emptying at the Santeetlah Powerhouse, approximately 5.4 miles upstream from Cheoah Dam.

Cheoah Lake begins immediately downstream from Fontana Dam's tailrace and accounts for approximately 595 surface acres. Unlike upstream Fontana and most other western Carolina highland impoundments, Cheoah is not a storage-type reservoir. Its limit capacity is quickly achieved whenever Fontana Dam's hydroelectric turbines are in operation. Extended periods of upstream power generation automatically mean receptacle turbine activity at Cheoah Dam.

Cheoah's headwaters are actually a tailrace river and are very productive during brief periods following turbine shutdowns at Fontana Dam. There is something magical about a tailrace river's descent following shutoffs. Aquatic insects (though scant) emerge regardless of the time of day and trout seem to come out of the woodwork. Fly-fishing streamers, dries, or nymphs or spinner fishing is good at this time, along with small spinners, floater/minnow plugs, and a variety of baits.

Limited natural reproduction occurs each spring in the Twenty Mile Creek drainage area. At this time many successful anglers concentrate their efforts along this narrow embayment and fishing near the bottom.

Trolling minnow-type plugs, dollflies, small spinners, or live bait is how many anglers convert otherwise slow angling periods into productive times. Most trollers use brisk speeds and concentrate on either the main river channel or close to the shoreline. Suspending bait in the tail of the boils at the Santeetlah Powerhouse is productive, but for safety reasons boaters should not get too close to this facility.

Shoreline fishing is very popular during the spring, particularly near the Twenty Mile Creek embayment and the Santeetlah Powerhouse, as well as along the highly accessible ways of US 129 and US 19.

There are no commercial docks or launches on Cheoah Lake, but there are two unnamed public launch ramps. The first, and most popular, is located on the north shore just down the lake from the US 19 bridge. The second is located at the Santeetlah Powerhouse, which is accessible from Tapoco via US 129. To reach the Santeetlah Powerhouse area, travel south on US 129 from its split with US 19, cross Calderwood Lake, and turn left onto Meadow Branch Road. At approximately four miles this gravel road arrives at the Santeetlah Powerhouse and ramp.

Tapoco is a very small outpost, primarily operated for Tapoco employees, families, and support personnel. Scona Lodge, a historical mountain hideaway, is located here, and although several attempts have been made to reopen this quaint turn-of-the-century establishment, at this writing I am sorry to say it is closed, with no reopening in the foreseeable future.

Camping is permitted along the lake's southern shoreline, which is held jointly by Tapoco and the Nantahala National Forest. Extended stays of over ten days are not advised, nor is littering, cutting down green or dead trees, and other related behavior. Many areas along the lake's southern shoreline are accessible only by boat and make a stay here quite pleasurable.

Calderwood Lake

Calderwood Lake is one of the South's least-known gems. Located between Cheoah and Chilhowee on the Little "T," this 536-acre impoundment offers superb trout fishing. Unlike its upstream counterpart Cheoah Lake, Calderwood offers more angling opportunities than just trout.

Bream fishing along the shoreline in Calderwood's lower end can be explosive during the summer months. Natural baits fished one to four feet deep are sufficient, but if your tastes are a bit more difficult to stimulate try using a popping bug.

Channel catfish are also abundant in this gin-clear lake, and while these fish rate high as table fare from almost all waters, whiskered fish from this clean lake are the mildest in flavor this scribe has ever eaten. Bank fishing for cats is productive, as are trotlines. Limb lining from the lakeside trees is loads of fun and when conditions are right will net more fish than two people can handle.

Calderwood Dam stands 213 feet high but is less than 200 feet across;

Calderwood Lake. Photo by Don Kirk.

during the summer this arch-shaped dam has the visual impact of a concrete wedge driven between two green sofa pillows. The lake is deep, with depths over 190 feet in the lower end along the river channel, which winds over eight miles back through rugged, remote ridges.

Like Cheoah, Calderwood Lake fluctuates, usually on a daily basis. The lake's level is dependant on upstream generating activity. Cheoah River enters the lake at its headwaters only a few hundred feet downstream from Cheoah Dam, although the two are unrelated.

Santeetlah Lake is created by the impoundment of the Cheoah River. If you're not confused now, add to this the fact that although the Cheoah River resurfaces downstream from Santeetlah Lake and is a "textbook" tailrace flow, it is not affected by power generated using Santeetlah Lake's stored water. This is accomplished at the Santeetlah Powerhouse on the south shore of Cheoah Lake.

Cheoah River drains a large section of the Nantahala National Forest. Other key feeder streams include Parsons Branch, a medium-size trout stream draining the Great Smoky Mountains National Park and Slickrock Creek, one of North Carolina and Tennessee's premier brown trout streams. This stream's 10,700-acre watershed is shared by the Cherokee and Nantahala National Forests and is protected by the U.S. Wilderness System.

The Tennessee/North Carolina state line bisects this lake less than two miles downstream from Cheoah Dam. A long-standing receptacle agreement between these adjoining states honors both states' fishing license on the entire lake and Slickrock Creek.

The lake's northern shoreline is National Park Service domain, and there is no roadside camping or designated backcountry campsite along Calderwood's length. The lake's southern shore is shared by the U.S. Forest Service (Nantahala and Cherokee National Forests) and Tapoco. Camping is permitted for reasonable lengths of time and under relatively liberal restraints on both properties, although commonly acknowledged courtesies such as no littering, permanent structure, large fires, cutting standing timber, etc. are required of those using these properties.

Calderwood Lake is the most remote and difficult to access of the Smoky Mountains Finger Lakes. Roadside access from US 129 is only available immediately downstream from Cheoah Dam at the two-lane highway's intersection with a gravel road which leads off US 129 to Calderwood Dam. The latter is a steep roadway difficult to pass during inclement weather. There are no marinas or other facilities on this lake.

Fishing pressure on Calderwood is light. Both Tennessee and North Carolina fishery departments stock this lake with brook, rainbow, and brown trout. Food is in short supply, but because fishing pressure is also scant, many of the lake's stocked trout live out their lives achieving considerable size. Brown or rainbow trout in excess of ten pounds are taken each year.

This is a bit ironic to those old-timers who remember when Calderwood Lake was created during the thirties. At that time fishery folks believed such high-elevation lakes could only be sterile, oxygen-depressed deserts, and this notion was carried over well into the TVA era. When Norris Lake was constructed during the mid-thirties, warm-water fish species hatcheries were also built to "hopefully establish some sort of fishery" in that 35,000-acre lake.

Following the impoundment of the Little Tennessee River at Calderwood Lake, no one checked to see if fish could exist in the lake — no one except the local fishermen who discovered that trout from the tributary mountain stream had migrated into the lake where they were growing fast and fat. For almost ten years the secret of this lake's excellent trout fishing was kept by a small group of anglers. When it was discovered that trout could live in tailrace rivers and deep mountain impoundments, regular stocking began here. To the chagrin of many local anglers, the quality of this lake's trout fishery actually dropped (in their opinion) due to the planting of fish from locales other than the mountain streams!

Fishing for trout at Calderwood Lake is very much like that at Cheoah, except during the summer these fish are deeper, often requiring the use of

The author fishing the tailrace of the Little Tennessee River below Fontana Dam. Photo by Joann Kirk.

a depth finder and downrigger when trolling, particularly in the lake's lower end. Night fishing in the lake's upper third is also popular and highly productive, not to mention lots of fun. One word to the wise: Even on the hottest August nights you can catch a nasty head cold in this frigid ravine!

When night fishing here, lanterns are suspended over the water and either spoons are vertically jigged or lively minnows still fished a few feet deep. Trout are very shallow at times or, for reasons unknown to this scribe, very deep. During the spring dry flies and terrestrial patterns are productive along the abundant tree-lined shore. Seeing a four-pound rainbow cartwheeling through a blooming redbud tree will certainly get your attention if the beautiful scenery around this highland lake hasn't already swallowed you.

Chilhowee Lake

The third "Finger Lake" is Chilhowee, a 1,747-acre impoundment of the Little Tennessee River and the only body of water in this group solely in Tennessee. Until the late seventies Chilhowee Lake was the final indignation borne by the Little "T" before emptying into the Tennessee River just downstream from Fort Loudoun Dam.

At that time, what was thought by many to be the finest trout river in the eastern United States was spawned beneath the shadow of Chilhowee Dam. Brown trout over seven pounds were common, as growth rates were excellent due to the rich limestone base over which the tailrace river flowed.

During the sixties TVA began the Tellico Project, and despite desperate efforts on the part of fishermen, conservationists, the Cherokee Nation, and others to stop and stall this endeavor, the project progressed and mournfully became a reality.

During the late sixties the famed snail darter was discovered in the Little "T" tailrace below Chilhowee Dam, and at that time was not known to exist in any other waters. This three-inch-long perch was quickly added to the federal Endangered Species Act list and for a time was both hailed and damned for halting this project. Ultimately, though, a slick congressional move by a Knoxville congressman permitted the side-stepping of the Endangered Species Act, and the freshly completed gates at Tellico Dam were closed, drowning forever this outstanding trout river. Many fishermen will long remember this majestic flow which soundly accounted for half of Tennessee's total trout water surface acreage.

I last fished that river only two weeks before it was killed. It was a bright autumn day, and we arrived just as the turbines at Chilhowee Dam were shut down. Our party of four caught almost 300 trout, releasing

A Chilhowee Lake trout.
Photo by Don Kirk.

many fish over 19 inches long. It was a golden farewell to a 24-karat trout river.

Chilhoweee Lake is the most diverse, accessible, and popular of the Finger Lakes. The dam stands only 68 feet high, but it backs up a lake over nine miles long. At its widest point, Chilhowee Lake is almost a mile across, five times wider than either Calderwood or Cheoah at their widest point.

This is a remarkably shallow mountain lake, seldom tapping over 50 feet deep, and usually less than 20, with 10-foot-deep water being very abundant along the shoreline. Chilhowee's headwaters are wedged between two vertical rock cliffs well worth boating up the lake to view.

Chilhowee Lake's primary feeder streams are Tallassee Creek, which enters along the south shore draining the Cherokee National Forest; Tabcat Creek, a minor Great Smoky Mountains National Park stream that creates a nice embayment area approximately five miles upstream from the dam; and Abrams Creek, a major Great Smoky Mountains National Park stream that enters the lake three miles upstream from the dam, resulting in a large embayment of Abrams and Panther creeks.

Chilhowee is actually two lakes: One is the coldwater trout fishery located in the lake's upper half, and the other a warm-water lake beginning around the mouth of Tabcat Creek. The cold-water fishery is maintained by the regular influx of icy, clean water from upstream Calderwood Dam.

Trolling for trout is popular and productive, as is night trout fishing which is practiced here just as on the upstream lakes, although by greater numbers of anglers. During the summer the lake is alive with lights as all sorts of fishing and pleasure crafts dot its course vying for tasty trout.

Fly fishermen will be delighted to discover that this lake offers season-long summertime long rod trout action in the trash line. Trash, or debris, lines beginning at the base of Calderwood Dam form from shoreline to shoreline. Viewed from above, these trash lines resemble "bath tub rings" as they slowly wash down the lake disappearing approximately five miles downstream.

These so-called trash lines hold large numbers of beetles, bees, and other terrestrial food that are of considerable interest to Chilhowee Lake's big rainbow trout. Trout cruise these trash lines, gingerly picking off insects. Fly flickers using large nymphs or beetle patterns sit in the bow of their boat or canoe and watch the lake's mirrorlike surface for an approaching feeder.

Once a trout begins prowling a debris line, it will follow it from one end to the other, rhythmically surfacing every 10 to 20 feet. The trick is to gauge your quarry's surface pattern and attempt to drop your fly where it will most probably surface again. Admittedly this is a hit-or-miss angling technique, but it can be awesomely effective. One nearby Maryville fly fisherman who has been flicking to the trash line trout for many years confided he took over 30 trout in excess of 20 inches from Chilhowee Lake in a single month!

Bluegill and catfish are abundant along the lake's lower half shoreline. Natural baits are the most popular way for taking these fish. Walleye are also found in this lake, and night fishing using jigs, spoons, and live minnows is the most productive means for taking these fish.

Chilhowee Lake is an excellent largemouth bass lake, although it is seldom noted as such. While fishing there in 1983, I saw one angler hook into a seven-inch stocked trout one afternoon, only to have a ten-pound hawg engulf the panicked trout. The bass was successfully landed by the fisherman.

Most bass fishing takes place downstream from the Tabcat Creek launch area. Top-water and spinnerbaits are recommended early in the season, while plastic worms and live baits work best following July. Little fishing takes place here during cold weather.

Chilhowee Lake sports no marinas, but it does have three public boat launch areas. The first is located at the mouth of Abrams Creek, the second is located one mile upstream from the first, and the third is located at the mouth of Tabcat Creek, five miles upstream from the dam. All three are easily visible from US 129.

Camping is permitted on the lake's south shore on properties owned by Tapoco and the Cherokee National Forest. Camping also occurs on the north shore downstream from the Panther Creek embayment area, but I cannot recommend this for two reasons. One, the area is gravel covered and virtually void of trees or other vegetation; and two, this area is frequented by thugs, hoods, and other unsavory sorts. I am at home around these gents and lasses, but anyone buying this book might certainly be otherwise.

Map Data

There are no individual maps of Cheoah, Calderwood, and Chilhowee lakes. A good map depicting Fontana and the Finger Lakes is available from the TVA by writing TVA Map Sales, 1101 Market Street, Chattanooga, TN 37402-2807, or by calling (423) 751-6277. USGS quadrangles of these lakes are as follows: Cheoah Lake—Fontana Dam, NC, Tapoco, NC; Calderwood Lake—Tapoco, NC; Calderwood, NC; Chilhowee Lake—Calderwood, NC.

Cherokee Indian Reservation
Public Trout Fishing

The public trout-fishing streams of the Eastern Band of the Cherokee Indian Nation in western North Carolina adjacent to the Great Smoky Mountains National Park rate among the most intensely managed waters in the United States. A total of 30 stream miles designated as "Enterprise Waters" by tribal leaders flowing through the Qualla Reservation annually provide thousands of fishermen with fun and trout.

Enterprise Waters are stocked twice weekly during the regular season (April through October) and weekly during the winter season (November through February). Creel-size (8 to 12 inches) rainbow, brook, and brown trout constitute the bulk of the Cherokee's regular season stocking efforts. However, just to keep things interesting, each week trophy-class 3- to 12-pound trout are released in all these waters. The present North Carolina state record brook trout, a 7-pound, 7-ounce beauty, was taken in 1980 from the Enterprise Waters portion of Raven Fork.

The Qualla Reservation's trout-fishing quality rates high. Summer creel limits are liberal: ten trout per day. Bait restrictions during this popular time slot are also virtually nonexistent. Naturally all of this bears a price tag.

Daily and seasonal user fees are charged of visitors, but presently, anglers fishing here are exempt from needing a state fishing or trout license. All things considered the cost of fishing at Cherokee is a red-hot bargain, especially if you're fishing for the frying pan or a trophy trout.

Revenue from fishing permit sales allows the tribe's fishery personnel to stock tens of thousands of trout annually. Until 1983 the Qualla Reservation was largely dependent on hatchery production from sources other than their own, primarily federal. Closure of a number of federal hatcheries forced the construction of a tribal fishery, which is located adjacent to Raven Fork on the Big Cove Road.

Bait fishing is permitted on all tribal Enterprise Waters open during the regular fishing season. Perennial favorites include such seemingly unlikely items as canned, whole-kernel sweet corn; miniature marshmallows; cheese balls; hot dog chunks; and even the shiny wrappers from sticks of chewing gum. The latter, according to Cherokee Fish and Game Management Enterprise Stocking Coordinator Adam Thompson, was the "secret" bait a youngster used a couple of seasons ago when he caught a trophy brown trout!

Other more natural baits proven effective for taking these trout include red wigglers, millworms, wasp larvae, minnows, hellgrammites, stickbait, grasshoppers, grubs, crickets, newts, and night crawlers. Many of these are available in a number of well-stocked bait shops located on the reservation.

Taking trout on bait is usually easier than opting for flies, especially for an inexperienced angler. Personally, I trout-fished for several years before taking up a flyrod (and then it took several years before catching trout via a fly!). In a nut shell, flies are seldom still-fished; they are almost always fished with the current. Bait is most productive when drifted naturally in the current, but it can also be allowed to sit on the bottom or even dangled in the current—and still catch trout. The latter two ploys are

Cherokee Reservation trout limits can include trophy-class rainbow, brown, and brook trout. Photo by Joann Kirk.

particularly noteworthy when high water prohibits most trout from finning in their favorite runs.

The tribe's three ponds open to the public are of interest, especially to those with young children or those unable to scamper around the rock-strewn creek banks. These ponds account for six surface acres and are located beside Big Cove Road, approximately five miles upstream from the town of Cherokee. They are encircled in well-manicured fescue grass and are heavily stocked twice weekly.

The three ponds are both productive and popular. Bait fished beneath a floater is the favorite ploy here, followed by the use of small spinners. Fly-fishing is not recommended around the ofttimes crowded pools for safety reasons. These ponds are also stocked during the winter trophy season, when large fish constitute most of the fish placed in the Enterprise Waters.

Several seasons ago during the winter season I'd been fishing Raven Fork upstream from the pond, where I'd limited out on 12- to 15-inch trout before returning to town via Big Cove Road by these ponds. Only one car could be seen in the gravel parking area there. Approaching that lonely vehicle were three frail-looking elderly ladies and one man. Each lady carried a rod and reel, but their male companion was burdened with what was without question the most impressive stringer of trout I've ever seen. On this stringer were 16 rainbow trout weighing between three and seven pounds each. Naturally I stopped to goggle and asked the expected question: "Whatcha catch 'em on?" One of the ladies produced her rod tip which held a single shanked hook with the body portion of a yellow jelly grup. Rubberized corn 'n' pond trout, the bane of me yet!

Streams presently under Qualla Reservation's Enterprise Waters designation include Raven Fork downstream from its confluence with Straight Fork, Bunches Creek downstream from where it passes under the gravel road, the Oconaluftee River from its entrance into the Qualla Reservation downstream to its boundary at Birdstown, and Soco Creek downstream from its confluence with Hornbuckle Creek to its mouth at the Oconaluftee River. All of these flows are tributaries of the Oconaluftee River and, with the exception of Soco Creek, all begin within the pristine confines of the Great Smoky Mountains National Park.

Raven Fork

SIZE: medium to fairly large

FISHING PRESSURE: extremely heavy

FISHING QUALITY: very good for stocked trout, outstanding odds for trophy-class trout

ACCESS: easily accessible via the Big Cove Road
USGS QUADS: Smokemont, NC; Bunches Bald, NC; Whittier, NC

Raven Fork leaves the Great Smoky Mountains National Park as more than a mountain rill; it rates as a small, fast-flowing river in its own right. This is one of the more popular "put 'n' take" streams, but one which, surprisingly, hosts a smart native population of rainbow and brown trout which many visiting anglers overlook for the easier food hatchery trout.

Raven Fork's upstream Qualla Reservation reaches are reserved for enrolled members of the Eastern Band of Cherokee Indians, but downstream from the creek's confluence with Straight Fork, public fishing is welcomed.

Big Cove Road, which begins at its junction with US 441 in the town of Cherokee, quickly traces alongside Raven Fork from its mouth at the Oconaluftee River to the starting point of Enterprise Waters at the mouth of Straight Fork, a distance of approximately eight miles. Big Cove Road is an excellent paved highway with a liberal scattering of commercial campgrounds and stores along its route.

While Raven Fork is a moderately wide, fast stream with an abundance

Ben Collins landing a trophy-class brook trout at the Qualla Reservation. Photo by Don Kirk.

of medium to shallow riffles, it also sports a large number of cascades and corresponding deep plunge pools.

Aesthetically, the Qualla Reservation portion of Raven Fork does not have the pristine, unspoiled splendor of its upstream national park headwaters. In all truthfulness, none of the heavily trampled Enterprise Waters are as pleasing to the eye as those in the National Park. This is not to say that Raven Fork or other Cherokee waters are not scenic, because they certainly are. However, complete protection is not afforded these streams and signs of usage can be found.

It is worth noting that 90 percent of Raven Fork (and other Enterprise Waters) flows very close alongside roadways that lend easy access.

There is a truism that also covers the stocking truck's twice-weekly deliveries. Newcomers curious as to where most of the best-stocked waters are located can make a "crack o' dawn" drive along any Enterprise Waters. Crowds, which always contain a cadre of regular long rods, will give you a blueprint to follow for future trips.

Should you make such a drive, you'll quickly see that less than 10 percent of the available water receives 90 percent of the angling pressure. Those lonely roadside ripples and apparently unproductive shallow runs are fished, but usually during secondary time slots, i.e., when results are suboptimum.

First, those areas void of crowds are usually not stocked as heavily, particularly those areas well off the road. In the out-of-the-way gorge-type runs, a certain amount of natural dispersal occurs, regularly bringing trout into these out-of-the-way locales. While some trouters disdain stocked trout, all will acknowledge that the longer a stocker survives in its new home, the more stream savvy it acquires and the more difficult it becomes to dube to a hook.

Raven Fork possesses a fair number of such remote, steep-bank gorges that require considerable effort to get into. These areas are not usually stocked but they hold amazing concentrations of sizable trout, particularly angler-wary browns.

Personally, I feel uncomfortable trout fishing in a crowd, or for that matter being in *any* crowd, be it in a liquor store or on a trout stream. Solitude is available on Raven Fork's off-the-beaten-path reaches, but don't expect easy pickin's 'cause Cherokee's trout streams receive considerable angling pressure and you're probably not the only fisherman who's drifted a night crawler along a difficult-to-access reach in recent memory.

One additional word of advice on the off-the-beaten-path stream reaches. Naturally one will try the most likely-looking runs and pools; everyone does. But if you want to up your catch rate, ferret your bait around unlikely-looking bankside structure and shallow midstream areas. Holdover trout many times become such creatures simply by virtue of taking up overlooked holding stations.

Bunches Creek

SIZE: medium to small
FISHING PRESSURE: heavy
FISHING QUALITY: excellent
ACCESS: fair; Bunches Creek Road, a four-wheel-drive-only gravel road
   traces alongside the Enterprise Waters section of Bunches Creek
USGS QUADS: Bunches Bald, NC

Bunches Creek is a medium-size tributary to Raven Fork which flows into the latter at the junction of Big Cove Road and Bunches Creek Road, a rough, four-wheel-drive-vehicle-only gravel road that connects Big Cove Road with the Blue Ridge Parkway, and then on to US 19W. That section of Bunches Creek downstream from the creek's last contact with the road (approximately 3.6 miles from its mouth) to its junction with Raven Fork is open to the public as Enterprise Waters.

Bunches Creek is one of Cherokee's most overlooked little trout-fishing hot spots. It is a small creek, but a very lovely bit of moving water. A constant overstory of hemlocks and hickories and a lack of crowds make this one ideal for an angler seeking a bit of elbowroom.

Bunches Creek has several noteworthy tributaries, most of which begin within the National Park, although not all by any means. These include Indian Creek (shown as Redman Creek on older maps), which begins at over 5,000 feet elevation west of the Heintooga Overlook on the western slopes of the Balsam Mountains in the Park and enters Bunches Creek approximately 1.3 miles upstream from its mouth. An old jeep road traces alongside Indian Creek, but under present tribal regulations, this stream is not open to public fishing.

Heintooga Creek, another high-elevation park flow, enters Bunches Creek approximately 2.4 miles upstream. This stream begins in the craggy area between Horsetrough and Heintooga ridges on the Balsam Mountains range. It is a pretty hop-across stream, which enters Bunches Creek at an elevation of almost 3,000 feet. Although the regulations given out by the Qualla Reservation Fish and Game Management Enterprise do not show this stream, it is restricted to tribal members only.

Oconaluftee River

SIZE: large
FISHING PRESSURE: extremely heavy, but rarely crowded
FISHING QUALITY: superb, particularly for large trout
ACCESS: excellent
USGS QUADS: Whittier, NC; Bryson City, NC

Fishing the reservation's reaches of the Oconaluftee River is a treat and would be even if it were not intensively stocked. This is one of the eastern U.S.'s great brown trout streams and one that shells out huge, full-finned "resident" trout with as much regularity as many western streams.

The Oconaluftee River is large enough to float fish from a canoe or johnboat during most seasons, although surprisingly few utilize crowd-beating methods. Most float trips occur downstream from the river's US 19 bridge.

Upon leaving the National Park the Oconaluftee River bisects the bustling tourist town of Cherokee, the Qualla Reservation's tribal center. Although one may be casting a Light Cahill in the shadow of a hamburger emporium, this does not really matter when the fish are biting. The river's roar and the delight of fishing bury all thoughts of civilization.

Fishing pressure is most intense where access is easiest: upstream from the US 19W bridge to the Park boundary. Conversely, the most intensive stocking occurs there and fishing is always excellent.

Angling pressure downstream from the US 19W bridge to the river's confluence with the Tuckasegee is scant, according to Adam Thompson, a longtime veteran with the tribe's fishery program and a member of the Eastern Band of Cherokee.

"Not many people fish down there because they don't think that area holds trout and access is a little more difficult. There the river is slower and looks deeper. This stops some from going downstream.

"This area isn't stocked as heavily as other easy-to-get-to places, but it does hold a lot of big trout, especially brown trout. Were I looking for a big trout, I'd try there, and I'd probably use a five- to seven-inch creek chub for bait, long-line fishing it into a deep, dark pool very early in the morning or in very late evening," notes Thompson. He has probably seen more fishermen catch the largest trout of their careers than any man alive.

Access to Oconaluftee River

US 441 traces alongside the river's eastern bank from the Park boundary downstream to the river confluence with Soco Creek. Big Cove Road lends access to the river's eastern bank downstream to where this road junctions with US 19W, which lends additional access to the Oconaluftee River downstream from the town of Cherokee to the reservation's boundary at Birdstown. Access to the river's other side is provided by a roadway known as Old #4.

Soco Creek

SIZE: small to medium
FISHING PRESSURE: heavy
FISHING QUALITY: excellent
ACCESS: very good
USGS QUADS: Sylva North, NC; Whittier, NC

Soco Creek is the only significant streamshed beginning within the confines of the Cherokee Indian Reservation. Its origins are between mile-high Soco Bald (5,440 feet elevation) and Waterrock Knob Mountain (6,292 feet elevation), a steep-walled series of ridges that divide Oconaluftee and Maggie valleys. Unlike its sister peaks to the west, Soco Mountain is home to many people, despite its rugged character and steep terrain.

Compared to other Qualla Reservation streams like the Oconaluftee River or Raven Fork, Soco Creek is quite small. Its headwater reaches are pleasant and tree-lined; however, its final three miles, though adequate and providing good fishing, lag behind other Cherokee streams in aesthetics. Soco Creek headwater reaches are small, but a generous helping of cascades and pools amidst the shade of towering streamside hemlocks and dense growing laurel make it appealing.

Soco Creek is large enough to permit fly-fishing, but well over 90 percent of all angling occurring here involves the use of natural baits. Redworms, cheese, doughballs, and corn are the premier baits with long-proven track records on this stream. Top spots include those deep pools (particularly those near the road or along a well-beaten path) and access road crossings. This is not meant to discredit other areas because they certainly hold large numbers of fish, especially "smart" holdover trout.

Upstream from Soco Creek's junction with Hornbuckle Creek, approximately ten miles upstream from its mouth at the Oconaluftee River just downstream from the town of Cherokee, this stream is restricted to tribal members. Although Soco Creek is fed by two impressive feeder streams, Wright and Jenkins creeks, these flows are not open to public fishing under the Enterprise Waters program. It is also worth noting that a very small section of Soco Creek downstream from the US 441 bridge to that point where the creek again flows adjacent to the reservation in places is partially under tribal control, while one section, approximately 50 feet, is under the control of the state of North Carolina. This area is well marked, but attention should be given that stream area when choosing to fish there.

Access to Soco Creek

Access to Soco Creek rates excellent, with US 19W providing the bulk of this access. This federal asphalt way closely follows the stream's course approximately 8 miles to the second bridge just upstream from the town of Cherokee. There the creek makes a 1.4-mile loop around a sloping ridge, skirting under US 441 before merging with the Oconaluftee River. There are no roads lending access to this loop area, but enough anglers explore it to keep a footway open along this reach.

US 19W follows Soco Creek very closely in most places, although it does lose sight of the creek in places. Numerous side roads lend additional access to those areas away from this highway and because Soco Creek, like all Enterprise Waters, is heavily fished, well-worn footpaths trace the creek's course.

Stream Index